LEADING
THE
CHARGE

ALSO BY GENERAL TONY ZINNI AND TONY KOLTZ
AND AVAILABLE FROM PALGRAVE MACMILLAN

Battle for Peace

LEADING
THE
CHARGE

LEADERSHIP LESSONS
FROM THE BATTLEFIELD
TO THE BOARDROOM

GENERAL TONY ZINNI
AND
TONY KOLTZ

palgrave
macmillan

LEADING THE CHARGE
Copyright © Tony Zinni and Tony Koltz, 2009.
All rights reserved.

First published in 2009 by PALGRAVE MACMILLAN® in the United States—a
division of St. Martin's Press LLC, 175 Fifth Avenue, New York, NY 10010.

Where this book is distributed in the UK, Europe and the rest of the world, this is
by Palgrave Macmillan, a division of Macmillan Publishers Limited, registered in
England, company number 785998, of Houndmills, Basingstoke, Hampshire RG21
6XS.

Palgrave Macmillan is the global academic imprint of the above companies and
has companies and representatives throughout the world.

Palgrave® and Macmillan® are registered trademarks in the United States, the
United Kingdom, Europe and other countries.

ISBN: 978-0-230-61265-5

Library of Congress Cataloging-in-Publication Data is available from the Library
of Congress.

A catalogue record of the book is available from the British Library.

Design by Letra Libre, Inc.

First edition: August, 2009
10 9 8 7 6 5 4 3 2 1
Printed in the United States of America.

To our kids:

Lisa, Maria, Tony, David, and Jonathan

CONTENTS

LEADING
THE
CHARGE

PROLOGUE

"A new dawn of American leadership is at hand." President Barack Obama spoke these words in 2008 after his historic election victory; they have been repeated often in news clips. Obama's charisma, superb oratory skills, high intelligence, youth, and racial heritage made him an exciting and appealing candidate, and they have inspired great hope for his presidency. But the excitement Obama generates goes much further than these personal elements. The expectation that he has brought new leadership to the nation and the world has tapped into a deep desire among Americans for true leadership in troubled and confusing times. I cannot remember an incoming president whose every statement was so intently listened to and examined. I cannot remember a transition that generated such attention to each and every cabinet and administration nomination down to the second, third, and even fourth levels. The interest in, fascination with, and scrutiny of the nominations to every major arm of government were unprecedented.

Why?

We are desperately searching for leaders who can deliver, not only in government but in every other region of our society. Never has a president come into power with such high expectations and hopes for his success.

Many of us have looked critically at the leadership failures and mistakes of the recently departed Bush administration with the mistaken belief that our country's problems will go away with its departure. It's no less simplistic to believe that the new Obama administration can right all wrongs. Our leadership problems go deeper than those of governance.

The end of the Cold War in 1989 radically changed the world; we are still reeling from its effects. For two decades we have confronted monumental and unprecedented change—a shakeup and reordering unlike anything we've faced since the end of World War II. The enormously varied and complex consequences of this change have confounded leaders everywhere. Their failures have been mounting, particularly in this second decade of the post–Cold War era, as the inability to understand and adapt to the messy and challenging new world has plagued us. These failures do not derive from a passing patch of bad leadership; nor can the new reordering be passed off as a temporary phase. We are, I hope, beginning to realize this.

This book is about the effects on leadership generated by the changes of the past two decades. It is about the leadership that has failed during those years . . . and about the leadership that is working. And it is a personal reflection on what I have learned and experienced about leadership and the tried and true principles that support it—principles too-often absent from today's leadership.

ONE

THE CRISIS
IN
LEADERSHIP

If you woke up today after a twenty-year-long Rip Van Winkle nap, you'd find yourself in a vastly different world from the one you had expected or hoped for—a shockingly changed world full of wild, scarcely believable crises, conflicts, threats, and turmoil. I'm certain that your first reaction would be alarm and horror. "What went wrong?" you'd ask. "Our nation and most of the world seemed to be sailing into calm, peaceful waters, not these storms." Outrage would quickly follow: "Who's been in charge? What happened to the leaders? How could they have led us *here?* Where have they been? What have they been doing?"

Those of us who have been awake during the last two decades are asking the same questions.

> Your government failed you. . . . We tried, but that doesn't matter, because we failed.

Richard Clarke, the former National Coordinator for Counterterrorism, directed these dramatic and emotion-filled words to the traumatized families of the 9/11 victims during his testimony on March 24, 2004, before the 9/11 Commission. His words shocked a TV audience of millions of Americans.

> Our investigation revealed that Katrina was a national failure, an abdication of the most solemn obligation to provide for the common welfare. At every level—individual, corporate, philanthropic, and governmental—we failed to meet the challenge that was Katrina. In this cautionary tale, all the little pigs built houses of straw.

These powerfully critical words came from the 2006 report of the eleven-member Republican House Select Committee investigating the Bush administration's response to Hurricane Katrina.

> From the passage of the resolution to overthrow Saddam to the failed attempts at reconstruction of Iraq, there have been so many missteps that the question of how we got into this mess has been obscured by finger pointing and blame shifting. The administration adopted a unilateralist policy, pushed it through a politically cautious Congress, and sold it through the lens of fear to the American people, who were inclined to trust their elected leaders in the aftermath of 9/11.

These are the words of respected Republican senator Chuck Hagel in his superb 2008 book, *America: Our Next Chapter.*

> America's generals have repeated the mistakes of Vietnam in Iraq. First, throughout the 1990s our generals failed to envision the conditions of future combat and prepare their forces accordingly. Second, America's generals failed to estimate correctly both the means and the ways necessary to achieve the aims of policy prior to beginning the war in Iraq. Finally, America's generals did not provide Congress and the public with an accurate assessment of the conflict in Iraq.

These damning words did not come from the media or an investigating commission but from a bright young Army officer, Lieutenant Colonel Paul Yingling, in an open letter in the *Armed Forces Journal* on April 28, 2007. Yingling's letter has subsequently resounded throughout the halls of the service academies and war colleges.

> When you see a corporation losing 40, 50% of its value . . . and then they fire their employees and sometimes even close their doors, and then the executives walk off with millions of dollars, how can you justify that?

These are the June 23, 2008, words of Representative Henry Waxman (D-CA), chairman of the House Oversight Committee, who has been examining CEO compensation and performance during the business and financial crises plaguing our economy.

> Obviously, the players who used performance enhancing substances are responsible for their actions. But they did not act in a vacuum. Everyone involved in baseball over the past two decades—commissioners, club officials, the Players Association, and players—shares to some extent in the responsibility for the steroids era. There was a collective failure to recognize the problem as it emerged and to deal with it early on. As a result, an environment developed in which illegal use became widespread.

This is one of the many criticisms of league leadership, from the Mitchell Commission's 2007 investigation into substance abuse in Major League Baseball.

WHAT'S HAPPENING HERE? You can't pick up a newspaper today without reading about some failure of leadership in virtually every segment of our society. Polls show that more than half of the American people are not proud of their nation's leaders, and three quarters say that without better leadership we are headed for decline. In its 2008 National Leadership Index, the Center for Public Leadership at the Harvard Kennedy School and the Merriman River Group released poll results showing that 80 percent of Americans believe that the United States faces a leadership crisis today—up from 77 percent in 2007 and 65 percent in 2006.

Lee Iacocca's passionate burn (in his 2007 book *Where Have All the Leaders Gone?*) powerfully articulates what most other Americans have come to feel: "Am I the only guy in this country who's fed up with what's happening? Where the hell is our outrage? We should be screaming bloody murder. We've got a gang of clueless bozos steering our ship of state right over a cliff, we've got corporate gangsters stealing us blind, and we can't even clean up after a hurricane much less build a hybrid car." Strong, blunt words that increasingly ring true with the American people. We expect far more from our leaders than we've been getting.

But it's not just Americans who worry about our leadership.

On a business trip to the Persian Gulf not long ago, I ran into an old friend, Pat Theros, who now runs an organization that promotes cooperative business relationships between the United States and Qatar. Back in the late 1990s when I commanded U.S. Central Command (CENTCOM), he'd been an exceptional ambassador to Qatar and a truly savvy Foreign Service officer whose political and regional insights I valued greatly. Since we both travel in the same circles—regional business, political, and military leadership—we compared notes. "Are you hearing the same thing I'm hearing?" he asked me. "I'm getting something from leaders out here that I've never heard before: 'We used to think you Americans were the best people in the world at getting things done,' they're telling me. 'Now we have doubts. You don't seem to be able to manage things well anymore.' I've *never* run into that attitude before."

"I've been hearing exactly the same thing," I told him. "A first for me, too."

These comments we were hearing were not gloating, sarcastic, or anti-American. They were expressions of genuine concern by prominent regional leaders who worried about the loss of respect for American leadership, action, and effectiveness. These Arab friends were not questioning American power but how our leaders were wielding it. And it wasn't just in the Middle East where I heard these kinds of comments.

Pat and I both had the opposite problem back in our earlier incarnations as Ambassador to Qatar and CENTCOM commander. In those days, our friends in the region used to think America was omnipotent: "If you Americans wanted to bring a successful outcome to the Middle East Peace process," they'd tell us, "you could broker and pressure a deal between the Israelis and Palestinians tomorrow." Or: "If you Americans wanted to straighten out the Iranians and tame their appetite for nuclear weapons, you could do it tomorrow." Or: "If you Americans wanted to take the sting out of Saddam Hussein and his thuggish regime and repair Iraq, you could do it tomorrow."

They had always looked up to us as the world champs at understanding problems and then directly and effectively handling them. If anything, they worried that we were sometimes too quick, powerful, and effective in our eagerness to resolve issues. For decades they'd seen us as the one nation in the world with the right stuff to manage any problem we faced. We were their wisest friend and partner . . . their beacon of freedom and understanding . . . the big brother—the benevolent global leader—they could put their trust in. Leaders out there often lamented to me that after World War II, we didn't extend to the Middle East the kind of enlightened reconstruction we had accomplished in Europe and the Far East.

Whenever we had these conversations with our political and military counterparts, we tried to inject a dose of realism: "Now wait a minute. Sometimes we've been smart, and we may be powerful in many respects, but we also have limitations. It's great that you have so much confidence in us. But we cannot resolve all issues as quickly and completely as you think or would like."

"No, no, no! You can do anything you want. America has all the necessary power, skill, and the influence."

Arabs are a proud people, with a rich culture, deep traditions, and their own ways of handling problems. Most Arabs accepted us as influential partners in the decades after World War II, replacing colonial or imperial masters. Most were very happy to have us standing with them, backing them up as a force of stability in the region. And most were confident that when we set out to get something done, it would get done. They, and the world, had witnessessed our half century of positive handling of a world war, a Cold War, and an economic boom.

Now all that had changed and for the first time they were openly questioning our motivation and competence: "Can you guys get it done anymore?"

They had seen us evolving into a blundering force of instability—an image many of our enemies love to reinforce and promote in the region and around the globe.

Middle Eastern leaders watching how we managed the 2003 invasion and occupation of Iraq may have had doubts about whether we should have gone in or not, but once we'd made the decision, they'd thought, "Well, in the end, the Americans will clean that up in short order." Instead, they saw us botch the occupation and get bogged down in a seemingly endless insurrection and civil war in which many thousands of civilians were maimed or killed and which threatened to destabilize their neighborhood. To Middle Eastern leaders, it was inconceivable that we didn't understand the forces we were unleashing through our careless intervention into the complex dynamics at play in Iraq, in Iran, and in the region.

Earlier they'd watched us kick the Taliban and Al Qaeda out of Afghanistan in a swiftly executed military operation. Then they watched us get distracted by Iraq. And then they watched Afghanistan stall and turn into a growing disaster. We're still chasing Osama Bin Laden and Mullah Omar after seven years of conflict. Instead of a quick resolution, we now have a dangerously growing cancer metastasizing into Pakistan and Central and Southeast Asia. Events like the recent Islamabad Marriott hotel bombing and the Mumbai terrorist attack threaten to ignite the entire region.

With increasing shock and anger, they have watched the humiliations and the torture under interrogation at Abu Ghraib and the controversial detainments at Guantanamo; and they were horrified to learn that Americans had stooped to "extraordinary renditions" to spirit away suspects to secret prisons in nameless countries without due process. This was not the principled and moral America they respected and thought they knew. For reformers and activists in the region, this fact was particularly troubling, since they held the United States up as the model for humane and responsible governance.

They'd watched the tragic unfolding of Hurricane Katrina and its messy aftermath—the rescue and cleanup from hell. Most Americans—but not our Arab friends—are unaware that the Emir of Qatar was the number-one contributor of aid for Katrina relief; other regional donors also assisted. Here was the United States of America, the richest and most powerful nation in history, and our own government's response to the disaster was so incompetent, inept, and foolish that we found ourselves welcoming aid from outside!

They'd watched our economy tank after the subprime mortgage crisis. According to our reputation, we had the best and most efficient financial system in the world, and yet it's hard to find a financial or political leader here who knew—or cared—that mortgage and other lending had gotten out of control. Loans that never should have been granted were bundled into financial instruments that were sold down some complicated chain of murky financial entities . . . and then bundled and sold again. A giant pyramid scheme: I don't know what else to call it. Worse yet, government agencies structured to monitor and regulate these actions seemed befuddled by the crisis and its depth.

"Where's the risk?" . . . "Who cares? Property values will never stop growing. Everybody makes money. Everybody's happy."

The hat-in-hand parade of American financial and industrial corporate executives going to Washington looking for taxpayer bailouts has been a public embarrassment for our nation and a cause of visceral anger for its citizens.

What do these stratospherically paid "leaders" have to say in their own defense? We expect them to explain clearly and reasonably how and why they led their firms, the nation, and the entire world into an economic catastrophe. They owe us a *clear* explanation of what went wrong. Instead they're offering up dodgy excuses. In an op-ed in the March 12, 2009, *New York Times,* financial author William D. Cohan provided a sample of statements from investment bankers whose organizations are now either dead or absorbed by more solvent ones:

> If I'd have known exactly the forces that were coming, [I'd have known] what actions . . .we [could] have taken beforehand to have avoided this situation. [But] I just simply have not been able to come up with anything . . . that would have made a difference to the situation that we faced.

These words were spoken by Alan Schwartz, the former chief executive officer of Bear Stearns, to the Senate Banking Committee in April, 2008.

> I wake up every single night thinking, "What could I have done differently? What could I have said? What should I have done?" And I have searched myself every single night. And I come back to this: at the time I made those decisions, I made those decisions with the information I had.

Dick Fuld, the former chief executive of Lehman Brothers, spoke these words to Congress in October, 2008.

Before their firms crashed and burned in 2008, Schwartz and Fuld were at the top of the investment banking food chain, with combined yearly incomes of only slightly less than $500 million. Were they blind, deaf, dumb? They had bet the futures of their firms on mortgage-backed securities and trades with hedge funds. At one time these relatively new tools in the banking toolkit had been enormously profitable—so profitable that these (well informed?) "leaders" had decided to largely ignore the less profitable but safer areas that had in the past sustained the banking business. Did it never occur to them that these newer tools carried titanic risks? How could they have failed to understand that if these investments tanked, their firms might not survive?

As our dismayed global friends watched America fumble, they wondered, "What happened to our wise big brother? What happened to the free world's great beacon of understanding, power, and freedom?" Thank God, their dismay hasn't turned them totally against us. Instead, they're truly hoping for an American renaissance, a return of the respected moral and competent leadership they admired. Like American citizens, they have a tremendous amount of hope that the Obama administration will turn the leadership crisis around.

Our enemies obviously enjoy watching and encouraging our missteps. They see opportunity in replacing the United States as the hyperpower, either globally (e.g., China) or regionally (e.g., Iran). In their view, their own flaws can be covered up by the attention and concern drawn to our failures. As one leader in the Gulf region recently told me, "The Iranians are running around here gleefully announcing the demise of America and capitalism. They tell us, 'I told you so.'"

NOT LONG AGO we were seen all over the world as "the indispensable nation," the sole superpower, an empire . . . but a benevolent empire of influence, without the negative legacy and history of empires of conquest and exploitation. Have our recent stumbles and falls made us a helpless, flailing giant? When we try to assert our leadership in the world, whom can we count on to follow us in future "coalitions of the willing"? Are we now a fading empire in terminal decline? Is it the end of the American century, as some have pronounced?

Make no mistake: we are not alone in this leadership crisis. Far from it. A June, 2008 WorldPublicOpinion.org poll of citizens from twenty nations found that none of the world's national leaders inspire confidence. It's almost as though an epidemic of diseased leadership has spread around the world and into every facet of global society.

What do perceptions like these mean for us now? Where must we go? What must we do? What is our place in these countries that once looked up to us? What is our place in the world? How did we let our place in the world plunge so precipitously? Where was the responsible leadership we count on to protect our citizens and to guide the nation into the future—an always risky and often dangerous process? . . . *Where were our leaders?*

IN THE UNITED STATES, few Americans will give encouraging answers to these questions. As I write, Americans are gloomier than they've ever been about our country's future. In a recent Gallup Poll, close to 90 percent of respondents were dissatisfied with the way things were going in America (up from just 30% in 2001).

They have a lot to be gloomy about.

The price of food seems to rise inexorably while the price of fuel swings wildly up and down without apparent rhyme or reason . . . even as home prices have taken a dive and credit has severely tightened.

(Seemingly ever-rising home values had been the credit prop for the economies of America and much of the developed world.) For most Americans, real incomes are either stagnant or falling. People who work in the private sector are losing health benefits. The quality of education in this country has plummeted. The nation's infrastructure is aging and falling down. Unemployment is on the rise, and retirement accounts have been in free fall.

Early in the summer of 2008, heavy rains in the nation's midsection overwhelmed our poorly managed flood defense system. Levees collapsed. Cities in Iowa and along the Mississippi were swamped. A major bridge collapsed in Minneapolis the summer before. Today, serious flaws in major bridges all over the country remain unrepaired.

The financier Felix Rohatyn opens his new book, *Bold Endeavors: How Our Government Built America, and Why It Must Rebuild Now,* with these tough words: "The nation is falling apart."

"Three-quarters of the country's public school buildings," he continues, "are outdated and inadequate. More than a quarter of the nation's bridges are obsolete or deficient. It will take $11 billion annually to replace aging drinking water facilities. Half the locks on more than 12,000 miles of inland waterways are functionally obsolete."*

Except in the Northeast corridor, passenger rail service in this country is a joke. The rest of the transportation system is aging and in danger of collapse.

The June 28, 2008, issue of the *Economist* reported: "Important gateways, such as the ports in Los Angeles and New York, are choked. Flight delays cost at least $15 billion each year in lost productivity. Commutes are more dismal than ever. Congestion on roads costs $78 billion annually in the form of 4.2 billion lost hours and 2.9 billion gallons of wasted gas, according to the Texas Transportation Institute."

---

*As quoted by Bob Herbert in the February 24, 2009 edition of the *New York Times,* which is also the source for the American Society of Civil Engineers information below.

According to the American Society of Civil Engineers, the nation must now invest $2.2 trillion over five years to get its infrastructure into acceptable shape . . . up from $1.6 trillion in 2005.

Our infrastructure is in dire need of repair and reconstruction. We look to our political leaders to fix these problems, but they have not acted. They seem paralyzed. When we most need exceptional competence and wisdom in allocating our shrinking resources, we've been getting political patronage and pork barrel earmarks. We've been getting "Brownie, you're doing a heck of a job." We've been getting bridges to nowhere and theme parks at taxpayers' expense. The expectations for President Obama and the Congress to change things are high. The preside nt faces monumental domestic challenges unprecedented in our history.

Beyond our borders, other looming challenges are shaping the future: climate change, the forces of globalization, the scramble for resources, failed and failing states, terrorism with global reach, humanitarian crises, the reordering of global power centers, the spread of weapons of mass destruction. Any—or all—of these challenges could quickly morph into crises with world-shaking effects.

What have our leaders done to take on these challenges? Do they even understand them?

True leaders get positive things done. That's their essential job description. They make sure that the institutions and organizations they lead are headed in a good direction, and they leave them better off than they found them.

Today there are too many "bottom-liners"—guys who are less interested in leading their people to long-term success than in trying to manage enterprises to quick, self-serving gain by manipulating processes and financial results. Such actions may work in the short term, but they will not sustain and ensure success into the future. Cheerleading organizations to success is also not enough. Stronger motivation and an improved work ethic are always good, but they will not get us through tough patches. We must deliver through competent and innovative leadership. In today's competitive world, "delivering" is much more difficult than it ever was in the past.

Today, too many leaders fail to get the job done. Too many fail to deliver. Too many fail to leave their organizations better off than they found them. How many Enrons or Tycos or Bear Stearns or Fannie Maes or Freddie Macs or bankrupt airlines or General Motors or Chryslers do we need to convince us that there is a problem in leadership? That too many leaders are not serving the interests of their enterprises, their stakeholders, or their employees? Do we trust our bank, our 401(k) manager, our congressman, or our employer to look after our interests?

Our nation's political and economic leaders seem impotent to address the challenges and crises that our nation faces. People are desperate. They want their leaders to do something; and our leaders seem confused or blind to what's going on out there . . . and helpless to deal with it. The recent presidential election was a cry for change and not for business as usual. In the quest for a new kind of leadership, Republicans nominated a maverick and the Democrats a political unknown. The debate between experience or change was interesting. Experience did not count for as much as one might expect. Were the people saying "Experience in old, ineffective ways won't get it done anymore. We'll gamble on untested change instead"? Our political system was not working. It had lost its way.

We need long-range answers to big problems. We need fresh ideas. We have not been getting them.

We have grown tired of the politics of attack ads and spin that produce no results beyond the electoral success of the perpetrators.

We want to trust some institution and its leadership with our future financial and security well being. But which one?

We want to trust our religious leaders, our community service leaders, our health care leaders, our academic leaders, and so on and so on. But can we?

Yesterday's methods of leadership, and of making leaders, don't work. They are failing us.

Fixes for these problems seem at best distant and hard, and will require sacrifices that Americans have not had to face in many decades. They feel tossed around by forces they aren't used to, and they fear what they can't control or understand. Who in America feels confident about the outcome of today's energy, financial, or climate change crises? Many have lost faith in our traditionally optimistic "can-do" attitude.

Has good old American "can-do" become "can't-do"?

No, we're not there yet.

But we face a dearth of the creative and innovative leaders who used to be the hallmarks of American leadership.

We have a leadership crisis!

So who's to blame? Where does the buck stop? Is it *just* a leadership problem? Will replacing leaders the way Lincoln replaced Union generals during the Civil War be the answer? Or is the problem deeper than that?

We can easily, and deservedly, pick on political leaders as the primary source of our discontent, but they aren't alone in inspiring discontent. People don't trust the media or business or religious leaders either. Poll numbers in all these areas have hit lows no less precipitously deep than Congress's or the former president's. Does anyone today have any illusions about the media? Does anyone think any news organization is truly objective and unbiased? Because all the media now come in political "flavors," all their reporting is suspect. Respected reporters with years of experience colluded with Bush administration message controllers. Religious leaders preach hate and bias from the pulpit and cover up intolerable sexual abuses and financial corruption. Candidates have had to distance themselves from, or disavow connections with, religious leaders who offered support. Once highly respected professionals such as doctors, lawyers, and bankers are now distrusted as greed, incompetence, and behavior scandals become far too frequent.

We have invested a lot in the hope that the new Obama administration will bring enough meaningful political change to justify Americans' hopes for real leadership. The Pope has apologized for the Catholic Church's sexual abuse scandal and has promised change. Professional sports league commissioners vow to clean up scandalous behavior and substance abuse by athletes. Our government regulatory agencies are bailing out financial institutions and claim to be on top of our flawed business practices. Our military is writing a new doctrine in order to cope with a different, unexpected kind of conflict. State attorneys general promise to prosecute political leaders, even governors, who abuse their office and trust. Our Congress continues to investigate failures in governance and corporate leadership. And so it goes.

All good stuff. But is it on the mark? Is it enough? Will it resolve our leadership crisis? Not easily. The problems, obstacles, challenges, and looming crises at home and all over the world are vast, systemic, pressing, and complex, and the actions taken so far seem reactive rather than curative.

Who comes out looking good? Once upon a time, the armed forces did. In the past, polls showed overwhelming support and respect for the military leadership. That's gratifying to know, given my nearly forty years of military service. The current reality, however, does not live up to the reputation. Even our most hallowed and valued institution, the U.S. military, has recently shown an alarming leadership drift:

In 2007, the *Washington Post* published a series of articles spotlighting the scandalous mistreatment of wounded vets at the Army's flagship medical facility, the Walter Reed medical center in Washington, D.C. Fallout from the scandal led to the forced resignation of Francis J. Harvey, the secretary of the Army, soon after he had relieved from command Major General George W. Weightman, the Walter Reed commander. Weightman was temporarily replaced by Lieutenant General Kevin C. Kiley, the Army surgeon general and a former Walter Reed commander . . . who was himself relieved of the command two days later.

Care for our wounded and injured vets is clearly a core issue for Americans. Nothing can, or should be, as sacred to us.

In the summer of 2007, Marine General Peter Pace, then chairman of the Joint Chiefs of Staff, was expected to be renominated and easily confirmed for a second two-year term. Instead, in anticipation of a contentious confirmation process in Congress, he was asked to step down. Congress had doubts about his leadership and handling of the Iraq war.

Early in 2008, the CENTCOM commander, Admiral William J. Fallon, resigned after his outspoken dissent from Bush administration policies in the Middle East sparked increasing tension between Fallon and the administration. Fallon's resignation added to an already eroding relationship between the uniformed military and the civilian leadership.

In the summer of 2008, Secretary of Defense Robert Gates fired the top Air Force leaders, Chief of Staff General Michael Moseley and Secretary Michael Wynne, after electrical fuses for nuclear warheads in ballistic missiles were mistakenly sent to Taiwan and a B–52 bomber had been allowed to fly over the American Midwest in 2007 armed with nuclear-tipped cruise missiles. (Because of the risks, the United States had stopped flying aircraft carrying nuclear weapons back in 1968—forty years earlier.) Questions about the oversight and control of our nuclear arsenal remain.

And I continue to be amazed at the silence and passivity of our military leadership—with few exceptions—during the run-up to the Iraq invasion in 2003. When Defense Secretary Rumsfeld and Vice President Cheney decreed that the invasion would be a walkover and the occupation would be a piece of cake, only one senior military leader publicly objected, Army Chief of Staff Eric Shinseki. When Shinseki warned that the occupation would require several hundred thousand troops, he was ostracized and driven into retirement. Unfortunately, his warning soon came true.

What were the other Joint Chiefs and senior commanders thinking when Shinseki was taking the heat from the Bush administration? Did they actually believe the Rumsfeld-Cheney doctrine that the occupation of Iraq would yield nothing worse than kisses and flowers? Why weren't senior military leaders willing to stand up for the truth, even if that meant throwing their stars on the table? Why did they allow the war to be conducted in a way that had major flaws obvious to the most junior officers and noncommissioned officers?

I'm not questioning here whether we should have gone into Iraq (though I have a view on that). I'm questioning how our leaders conducted the invasion. They threw away CENTCOM's carefully prepared war plan, substituting a poorly thought out, seat-of-the-pants fantasy. They went in with too few troops—enough to take down Saddam's regime, but not enough to secure the country afterward. They didn't expect that our military would be involved in the reconstruction; yet the military got stuck with it, as usual. Our leaders' military decisions didn't stop the looting, didn't protect the borders, didn't put a lid on the insurrection, didn't prevent the needless deaths of thousands of American servicemen and women and tens of thousands of Iraqis. Military commanders should have seen how their decisions would impact the Iraqi people, their own forces, and their military missions. They should have seen that they were allowing operations to be conducted in a way that endangered the mission and their troops. And then they should have forcefully sounded the alarm. As Senator Jim Webb (D-VA), an experienced combat veteran, said, in a February 6, 2007, statement on the Senate floor: "it was predictable—and predicted."

A few years ago, the young Army officer (now general) H. R. McMaster's brilliant and influential book, *Dereliction of Duty,* accused the Vietnam-era military leadership of passivity and silence in the face of the Johnson administration's strategic hubris. Because today's military leaders have not learned from these failures, they've fallen into the same pit. That is why Lieutenant Colonel Yingling's open letter hit home to so many in uniform.

Obviously I can go on and on citing leadership failures in every endeavor; but clearly, that's not necessary. The case is being made all too frequently, every single day, as leadership failures are reported and analyzed, and the people who suffer the results are polled.

But why is leadership failing?

Does the crisis in leadership have a central single cause in some deep flaw in today's American society—in education, in the makeup of the people, in a fading away of our moral fiber, in a decline in national will, in the way leaders are made, or in some other tumor that is metastasizing into the military, the government, business, the clergy, and sports? Are we looking at a single failure? Or are we looking at multiple causes?

And are we in fact looking only at an American failure? Or is the failure perhaps broader? Might it be worldwide, as the polling suggests?

In my view, the causes of the crisis are not simple, and the crisis is not limited to the United States. The causes are complicated. The crisis is worldwide.

You can't just take a good person, a good *potential* leader, and throw him or her into a dysfunctional briar patch and expect success. We have bad, outdated business models in too many industries. Look at the airlines. Is anyone actually eager to go out to an airport, go through the ticketing, security, and boarding grinder, get on an airplane, and fly somewhere? Look at the American automobile industry. It can't compete with its foreign competitors and has lost the trust and confidence of the American consumer.

Throwing potentially good leaders into these situations without changing the model is a recipe for repeated failure.

Today's world is vastly changed from the world of twenty years ago—vastly changed from the world that leaders worldwide grew up to understand. These changes have forced leaders to face, understand, and master a complex confluence of swiftly morphing events, conditions, and circumstances. The crisis of leadership starts, at its heart, as a crisis in adapting to the new world.

TWO

THE FAILURE TO ADAPT

In the summer of 1992, I returned from a two-year assignment in Europe, still trying to comprehend the end of the Cold War and the myriad other astonishing events I had witnessed in Europe, the Middle East, and the former Soviet Union. My new position excited me: I was to be Deputy Commanding General at the Marine Corps' Center at Quantico, Virginia, which was responsible for developing concepts and doctrine and educating our leaders. I couldn't have asked for a better assignment, and I couldn't wait to settle into it. All of us in the Marine Corps leadership sensed that we were embarking on a new era; at this post, at this time, the best thinking about all this change—and its implications for my service—was occurring.

But first I had more mundane tasks to perform—the routine tasks of resettling a family after years of living abroad. Every service member knows these issues well.

After moving into my family's assigned base quarters at Quantico, I set out to buy a car. For years (until my overseas tour), I had bought my cars from a friend, a retired Marine, who ran a dealership nearby. I headed off to his lot. When I pulled in, the huge neon sign above the showroom gave me a big shock. It now read: HONDA. When I'd left the United States, his dealership had sold Chevys. I had always bought American: Chevys, Fords, Dodges. What was happening?

The instant I walked in, my buddy, Bob, rushed over to greet me. After a quick hug and an exchange of updated family info, I said,

"Bob, you communist, how could you sell cars that aren't American?" With a laugh, he took me over to a Honda, opened it up, and pulled out a certificate stating that the car had been built . . . in Ohio. He then showed me a *Consumer Reports* rating that placed Honda's performance and reliability far ahead of the competition. The ratings clearly put American cars at the bottom of the heap.

"Take a look at the 'American' cars at any of the other local dealers," he told me, "and check to see where they're made."

I took him up on his challenge.

At my first stop, I learned that all the "American" cars on that lot had been assembled in Mexico. I was shocked. "What's an American car now?" I asked myself. "Do we determine the answer to that question by the location of the corporate headquarters? Or by where the plants and jobs are located? Or by the nameplate—Chevrolet, Chrysler, Ford?"

Answering that question today is still confusing. When I recently checked online, I found this rule: If 75% of a car's parts are made in the United States, then that car qualifies as American made. It turns out that under this rule, several familiar "American" cars—Dodge Rams, for example—do not qualify as American.

I went back to Bob and bought the Honda. But my confusion remained.

What I was experiencing was the impact of growing economic globalization. Not surprisingly, multinational corporations had been quick off the mark to jump into the wide-open and changing world I had seen emerging in Europe after the Wall came down. As I found out shopping for cars, things were not just changing in big political and security ways, they were changing in ways that touched the most ordinary and daily parts of our lives.

1918, 1945, AND 1989 . . . years of *big* change. They not only marked the end of three wars, two hot and one cold, they launched seismic shifts in the global environment—world-shaking transitions in political, security, economic, and social systems. The effects generated by these changes unfolded through many dimensions—in technology, in economics, in the means and techniques of production, in the use and availability of resources, in the conditions of labor, in the relations among nation-states, in their internal governance, and in the threats out there in the world—and created openings for the formulation of new sets of global rules and systems and new world environments.

Unlike the environments that emerged from the two world wars, the one that followed the 1989 collapse of the Soviet Union did not rise out of the ashes of a global war. Yet the post-1989 changes have been no less vast, comprehensive, and ongoing.

The two earlier global reorderings were followed by decades-long periods of consolidation and development. We are now well into the second decade of the current reordering and see no end to astonishing, rapid-fire changes which have generated new and ever greater security and economic challenges (these changes were extensively discussed in my 2006 book, *The Battle for Peace*). The biggest of these changes has been globalization in all its many and complex manifestations.

Globalization has produced new international interactions and the breaking down of borders, a global explosion of information technology and information access, mass migrations and the identity issues they create, chronic plagues of violence, the shift of world power bases, failures of governance and economic systems, the rapid urbanization of rural societies, the unchecked abuse of the environment, and the rise of borderless nonstate entities—good ones and bad ones: drug cartels, NGOs, charitable organizations and foundations, terrorist networks, and multinational corporations.

These and many other emerging forces are generating a more diverse and seriously stressed global society. Failed or incapable states have become bases and sources for problems with global impact. Humanitarian crises are increasing in scope and frequency. Economic systems are in turmoil. Powerful nonstate entities are increasingly replacing the traditional nation-state system, confusing old concepts of identity and authority.

Ever more changes have been swirling into this turbulent confluence of events and phenomena. Swarms of new forces have rushed into the vacuum opened by the collapse of the old structures. They have whirled around unchecked, gathered strength, shot out in unexpected directions, and now form a perfect storm that has left our leaders struggling to understand what's going on—much less to control events and influence conditions.

Maybe because this reordering was not set off by a big bang but by a subtle deflation of the Soviet superpower's might; maybe because the changes are so numerous and relentless in their coming; maybe because they are impacting virtually every facet of the world's ways of functioning—whatever the reason(s), leaders seem trapped in the past order and helpless to act effectively in the new one. At times they seem overwhelmed and in denial even of its very existence. They have been unable to adapt.

LIKE OTHER SENIOR RETIRED OFFICERS, I am often asked to participate in sessions to review and critique concept papers that look at the ways our military forces will fight and operate in the future. These are usually developed by Pentagon staffs, and are designed to drive doctrine, the procurement of military equipment, training, and all the other components that make up our military structure. We retired generals and admirals serve as "graybeards" who presumably offer sage and experienced views. Before we jump into these sessions with our own thoughts, ideas, opinions, or recommendations, we are briefed by intelligence experts on the latest thinking about future trends and the security environment in the years ahead.

Not long ago at one of these reviews, I was particularly struck by the opening brief on the future environment. As the briefer rambled on, several of his predictions about the world, ten years or so hence, grabbed my attention. I wrote them down:

- The defining attributes of the future operating environment will be uncertainty, complexity, and potentially rapid change.

- Events will be fundamentally unpredictable and sometimes counterproductive.
- Friction and uncertainty will abound.
- Accidents and miscalculations will be common.
- Negligible events will produce disproportionate and often unintended consequences.
- Strategic surprise will occur.

The briefer's intention was to paint a picture of the world our military will face years into the future. But what struck me was that he was *not* describing the future; he was describing today! The conditions he was ascribing to a future world have in fact been unfolding since 1989.

The world didn't begin to change on 9/11; it began to change twelve years before. The events of 9/11 should have been a wake-up call, one of many. The mess in the Balkans in the 1990s, the surging migrations of desperate people, the rapid realignment of economic power, the volatile ongoing transformation of the Islamic world, and many, many other signs of profound change have been erupting all around us ever since the Soviet empire collapsed.

I'VE SPENT MOST OF MY adult life "over there," in the eye of some storm or other. For forty-plus years, I have seen the world in its raw, unfiltered state.

During the first half of those four decades, I saw a world of reasonable order and predictability. The conflict between the two superpowers was always dangerous and full of risks, and wrong moves could have left most of the planet a smoking, radioactive cinder. One misstep or miscalculation could be devastating. Yet change came in measured bites that could be easily digested. Borders, geography, and walls defined us. Competition between the two big powers played out mostly in Third World countries in ways that would not threaten a wider confrontation. The bipolar power structure drove just about everything and imposed a comprehensible order and control.

In those days, we understood the world politically, economically, militarily, and socially. We basically understood how to approach it, what we had to do, and how to take on and solve the problems we faced. For fifty years we knew how to deal with communism and the Soviet Union: deter and contain it. And we built a strategic design that accomplished that aim.

The second half of my career saw an increasingly disordered, high-speed, dangerous, and surprise-producing world.

I was there when that new world was launched. I stood at a vacant Checkpoint Charlie and watched euphoric Berliners chip away at the Berlin Wall in happy frenzy. I knocked off a few chips myself. The expectations, the emotions, and the sense of relief and promise radiating from that epicenter in Germany were palpable. The long nightmare was over. The Doomsday Clock was set back. The world was saved. A new era of peace and progress had begun. A *Time* cover from those days picturing presidents George H. W. Bush and Mikhail Gorbachev above the headline "New World Order" seemed to say it all. Most world leaders were confidently declaring this new world order, along with the peace dividends and prosperity that went with it. Even the Secretary General of the United Nations was touting his new "Agenda for Peace."

Yet as I observed events from that same German epicenter during the next few years, I grew to see that those hopeful proclamations were premature.

What happened?

In my last years wearing a Marine uniform, I saw a world changing in ways no one had imagined. From the U.S. European Command in Stuttgart, from the hills in Kurdish Northern Iraq, from the streets of Mogadishu, from government offices in Moscow, from the deserts of Arabia, and from many other places all across the globe, I witnessed a world spinning on a different axis from before. It was not spinning into order, peace, and ever greater prosperity. It was spinning into disorder, confusion, and growing chaos.

After I retired in 2000, in my new roles as a diplomat, peace mediator, businessman, and teacher, I saw the ever-rising pace of change and the ever-growing disorder from the rice paddies of Aceh, the boardrooms of Dubai, and the jungles of Mindanao, and in lecture halls at international universities and mediation sessions in Geneva and Jerusalem. I have directly and personally experienced the radical changes generated by the new world in all its complexities. Those of us witnessing these dynamic events were increasingly mystified by the dissonance between the realities we saw and the hopeful but empty words we were hearing from our leaders. They were telling us that everything was okay, that we could keep on doing business as usual, that we could sail through the coming days with old models and methods. But the forces that provided order and control were gone. The lid was popped. We could see it. Why couldn't they?

The conditions that were emerging were perfectly visible to anyone willing to pay attention. At the three key hinges of change in the last century—1918, 1945, 1989—our country's presidents, Wilson, Truman, and the first Bush, recognized they were facing new conditions, and each tried, with varying degrees of success, to shape the changes and conditions in play.

Woodrow Wilson tried to warn of the need to influence a changing world, but his warning went unheeded. Harry Truman, George Marshall, George Kennan, and other great American leaders recognized the challenges and successfully addressed them. George H. W. Bush saw the new world coming but failed to realize that it would not order itself. And now, twenty years later, we're still waiting for the new world order he had promised. How many of our leaders are making the same mistake? Look around. The new world requires new ways to lead. Where are the leaders who are taking us into that new world?

WHAT WENT WRONG? Why do leaders in government, in the military, in business, and in other elements of our society fail to understand the changing world and how to operate effectively in it?

In my view, they haven't understood or adapted to the changes because the changes were too many, too fast, too diverse, and too unexpected.

The withering away of the Cold War meant we had dodged a world-devastating hot war. And the world that then emerged initially appeared far more stable and capable of self-ordering than it turned out to be. All that great news so dazzled American leaders that they did not see the lightning development of technologies and the speedy scramble of millions of desperate and newly empowered people in the world to grab a better life; they did not see the new generation in our own country produced by these changes; and they failed to adapt:

1. They tried to manage complex, fast-morphing challenges with simple, tired, habitual, linear methods and approaches. They missed the depth of complexity and the understanding that old processes and models didn't work anymore.
2. They lost the ability to look and plan ahead. They had no vision. They were trapped in rigid bureaucracies, buried in the details and the here and now. They failed to think strategically—a lost art in these new times.
3. They were reactive rather than innovative. They failed to be creative and forward-acting.

Doing business has never been easy, whether you're trying to run a hardware store in a small town in Massachusetts or to manage difficult negotiations between powerful, competing nation-states at the United Nations in New York. Complexity goes with the territory.

So when I say that the world of the twenty-first century is complex, I am not saying that the twentieth-century world was simple and easy to manage. It was anything but. I'm saying that there are differing levels of complexity and confusion and differing rates of change—differing tempos. The challenges faced by our Cold War leaders were tough and dangerous and fraught with horrendous consequences. The challenges we face today may be arguably less globally frightening, but certainly they are far more rapid, complex, and confusing.

We say that the world has "shrunk" or "flattened"—because of advances in transportation and communication and the emergence of new world economic powers, such as China, India, South Korea, Brazil, and a resurgent Russia. This shrinking has not resulted in simplification. On the contrary, we all face more challenges every day than we want to handle. There's too much information, too much interdependence, too much speed, too much competition. Though many leaders advocate a return to political, economic, and cultural isolationism, you can't walk that cat back. You must deal with conditions as they are.

Not too long ago, I was asked to talk to a gathering of food producers and distributors in the Midwest. The subject of my talk was the importance of analyzing and understanding the business environment—what I call "the sea you swim in." I was making the case that in this day and age, even small businesses have to work in a much more universal environment than ever before, and they better understand it.

After my talk, someone in the audience came up to me. "Boy, did that resonate with me," he said. "I have an old, family-owned food distribution business. When my father ran it and when I came into it, I could geographically draw for you my environment, my sphere of operations, my suppliers, my customers. All of these were confined to a small area in the Midwest—very narrow, contained, and definable. Now I have suppliers from all over the world. I ship foodstuffs all over the world. I do my distribution networking system and my administration through companies in India. When you call in and place an order, you have to go through Bangalore. If I map my small business today, it's increasingly global in almost every respect."

What's the difference between the operations and practices this man employs now and when he took over his business from his father? What does he have to understand now that he didn't have to understand then?

He has to understand global politics, global communications, global distribution systems, global markets, and global suppliers. He has to understand technologies he had never heard of when he took over the business. His one-time simple, comfortable, easily mapped world has turned messy, confusing, ever-changing. He had looked forward to a future that continued the proven ways his father had pioneered, when it was enough to be an expert at producing food and putting it out to market. Instead, he ran into an explosion of complexity.

The George W. Bush administration ran into a similar explosion when they invaded Iraq in 2003. Mere weeks into the invasion, when they thought they were winning, they celebrated victory on an aircraft carrier, where the president gave his infamous "Mission Accomplished" speech.

Everything was going great . . . and then somehow something went terribly wrong. As Defense Secretary Rumsfeld put it: "Stuff happens."

How did the most powerful military force in the history of the planet get bogged down in a third-rate country? What happened?

Those of us who have a long familiarity with the Middle East had this answer: "You were losing from the time you crossed the line of departure (the line from which an attack is launched). You allowed yourselves to get lured into defining success simply as a quick march to Baghdad that took down the old regime. That was not the real battle. We had always understood we could do that in a few short weeks.

"What you did not understand was that you were unleashing forces in Iraq and in the region that would consume you from the day you entered that country. You were caught up in the illusion of the short-term victory. And you failed to look at, much less understand, the strategic perspective. When you did not secure Iraq's borders, when you did not secure the population, when you rolled back any form of traditional authority, when you pulled the plug on a government that had dominated the economy and most other aspects of Iraqi society and culture, you opened the gates that set free the long-brewing demons of religious and ethnic intolerance that sparked a firestorm of looting, destruction, and ethnic violence. You didn't see the true complexity in that society, and the complexity came back and bit you."

When the war was just kicking off, I was on a business trip in the Gulf region. Everyone I met was shaking his head over the naive comments in the American media. The pundits were all gushing about how Americans would be greeted in Iraq with "flowers in the streets," about how the transformation of Iraq would be a "cakewalk," and about how the "liberation" of Iraq would inevitably lead to the "liberating" and "democratization" of the other countries in the region. And, oh, by the way, Iraqi oil would pay for it all!

One evening I was watching events unfold on television with Middle Eastern friends. President Bush was making a speech in which he pronounced, in essence, that the war was about the forces of democracy and freedom against the forces of authoritarian dictatorship. As he was speaking, one of my Arab friends leaned over and said, "No. It's about Sunni against Shia. You unleashed the devil." And then another Arab said, "No. It's Persian against Arab. You unleashed another devil."

They were all right—even President Bush. The invasion was about freedom versus dictatorship, but it also unleashed all those devils my friends mentioned. If I have an objection to President Bush's comment, it's not for missing the target; it's for missing its multilayered depths and the second- and third-level consequences to his actions. He saw conditions in Iraq and in the region in the simplest, easiest-to-grasp terms, in one dimension only. In his mind this was a simple liberation, not a complex occupation. He missed the complexity of the situation.

Let's say I'm a chemist working to shape a complex chemical compound for use in some industrial process. One of the many elements in that compound has a negative impact on the process, so I want to change or neutralize that element. "How can I make the change simple and easy?" I ask myself. "Maybe I can add another element to the compound that will neutralize the one that's giving me problems." Or: "Maybe I can replace it with some other, more beneficial element." So I try one of those simple solutions . . . and discover that my change reforms the entire nature of the compound—for the worse. My simple solution doesn't do what I wanted it to do. Instead, I've created another problem. I did not consider deeply enough the complexity of my compound. A simple, single-layered analysis may yield a well-intentioned application that alters the entire system in a major way. Unless we analyze the total system holistically, the pesticide we choose to apply to gain more crop yield may damage the entire ecosystem.

You can't apply simple, linear approaches to complex systems.

Back when I was commanding CENTCOM, we had plans for the invasion of Iraq. These plans—contrary to Rumsfeld's later charge that they were "old and stale"—were up to date, dynamic, and thoroughly rehearsed, revised, and reviewed from a military perspective.

As I analyzed our plans, it hit me that we had a problem. We understood the military dimension. We understood how to defeat Saddam's army, his Republican Guard divisions, his air and ground defenses, and so on. But something else was bothering me—partly because I was hearing it from friends in the region, and partly because I had learned it from my own experience going back to Vietnam. I realized that if we ever had to intervene in Iraq, we were going to be challenged by conditions that were far more complex than a military problem. I knew that driving up to Baghdad, defeating the Republican Guard, and pulling the plug on the regime was not going to be the end of that story. The operation was not going to be that simple or linear. There was more to it than that. My own intuition and experiences were telling me this. My friends in the region were telling me this. My own study of Iraqi society and the forces at play there were telling me this. And my commanders and staff were telling me this.

I knew that I was not expert enough to come up with and define the specific and concrete answers we had to have, so I asked for an analysis in the form of a war game, which we called Desert Crossing, to gain these insights and provide understanding of the level of complexities we faced beyond the military dimension. Because I was convinced that the social, economic, political, and other nonmilitary issues we faced were going to cause us the greatest problems, and because those were the issues that I least understood, I particularly wanted the nonmilitary agencies in our government to participate. Invading Iraq would force us to rebuild, virtually from scratch, a fragile and unnaturally created society while unleashing all sorts of forces trying to rip it apart. The military would have a difficult enough time handling security; who would handle the rest? From what I could see, the rest was where we were going to run into the big problems.

Desert Crossing gave us the opportunity to hear from every available source with knowledge of Iraq and Iraqi society. Using this rich database, we built scenarios covering every possible outcome once the lid was popped on the Saddam regime.

The exercise proved to be both a confirmation and a revelation: "My God!" I said to myself. "Our initial perceptions and judgments were right." But the reality went much deeper than that. The exercise showed that Iraq was even more complex and multidimensional than we had thought. It was absolutely clear to me that running up and taking Baghdad was not going to be our real problem after an invasion. It would have been only the first of our problems. I remembered a talk that the then Speaker of the House, Newt Gingrich, gave to a number of us at the National War College. He said, "When your political masters give you what they see as a seemingly simple task, always ask, 'And then what?'" After the invasion of Iraq, our real problem was going to be "And then what?"

It was clear that if we marched to Baghdad and tossed out the thugs who were the only source holding this very fractious nation together, Iraq would come apart. We would have to control the country and rebuild it, and that would require a lot of troops.

In 2000 I left CENTCOM and retired.

Fast forward to 2003. The United States invaded Iraq. Our military made short work of Iraq's forces—as we all knew it would. But what then? The dreaded "o" word—occupation—which the Rumsfeld Pentagon did not accept or understand, was our only choice if we wanted to stabilize the country. And then, once we made that choice, who would manage the occupation? The military could handle the security pieces, but what about all the other pieces? Who was going to handle the nonmilitary parts of an occupation? Who would be the "viceroy"? Who would take charge of rebuilding the infrastructure? Where was the plan for all that?

The rest of the story, as they say, is history; and historians will almost certainly judge that this adventure was a classic case of twentieth-century leaders failing to understand the complex twenty-first-century world they were living in.

If we don't understand this new world, then we will not understand how to survive, thrive, and prosper in it. If we fail to adapt, fail to innovate, fail to develop and grow, we will find ourselves forever reacting and struggling. How do we adapt? When do we realize that the old models do not work anymore?

THE MILITARY OF THE Greatest Generation fought World War II. They were skilled adapters and innovators. At the beginning of that war, our armed forces were inferior in every way to those of our enemies. German and Japanese equipment, numbers, combat power, and training were in almost every case better than anything we had to throw against them—German Panzer tanks and airplanes, Japanese Zeroes and ships were all technologically superior to ours.

Three and a half years later, we dominated every aspect of combat. Our technology and equipment were totally superior. We had overwhelming force. From a very small army—at the start of World War II, ours was nineteenth in the world in terms of size, with no large units—we produced leaders like Marshall, Patton, Bradley, Eisenhower, MacArthur, Hap Arnold, Spaatz, Stilwell, Nimitz, Vandergrift, "Howlin' Mad" Smith, and many other top leaders who came to command, maneuver, and operate large forces on a scale never seen before. We grew to that capability in *only* three and a half years.

The Germans had been developing their military prowess over a much longer time, and from a much deeper history, with a much larger investment in wealth, energy, and commitment.

We adapted.

We are a nation renowned for adaptation and innovation, not just in our military. In the past, America's entrepreneurial business leaders built a powerful economy, brilliant strategists formed our policies, and creative social leaders shaped our society to meet the changing times.

Leaders like George Marshall, who had a brilliant sense of the world and a prescient sense of the future, are no longer rewarded and valued in the very reactive society that is today's America. George Marshall was a deep and thorough thinker, a man of substance. He was *not* a "sound bite" guy.

We have become a "sound bite" society, demanding instant gratification and simple solutions. We suffer from a collective attention deficit disorder that won't permit us to think in complex, long-term ways. We no longer value strategic thinking. It's boring. A presidential debate is decided by a clever phrase or tomorrow's bumper sticker rather than deep discussion. A one-page policy paper by an inexperienced think tank fellow is adopted as a solution to complex international problems. A financial crisis is handled by a quick government bailout. But these reactive solutions can't work in this day and age.

"Where are the George Marshalls?"

In our chaotic times, all of us are looking for him. We hope a man or a woman for the times will emerge—a man or a woman who "gets it."

Today that "it" is tremendously difficult to "get."

The new environment created by the collapse of the old order has made it hard for leaders to lead successfully.

This is not solely an American problem; this is not a lack of strong potential leaders problem; and this is not an absence of desire to lead problem. It's an understanding and adapting problem.

Are any leaders adapting to the changes?

Sure. Absolutely.

New leaders are emerging who *do* get it—not many of them, hardly a flood . . . a few. What's different about them?

A great deal.

THREE

THE NEW LEADER

For two tough summers between college semesters, I trained to be a Marine officer in Quantico, Virginia, the home of the Marine Corps Officer Candidate School. Julys in Quantico were as hot and humid forty-seven years ago as they are today. The oppressive weather just added to the stress put on us by starched and ramrod-straight Marine noncommissioned officers (NCOs) who controlled our lives 24/7.

Amid the sleepless blur of close order drill, physical training, weapons firing, and field exercises, one event has stuck in my memory—the Leadership Reaction Course. The LRC—light-years different from everything else we did—was my first experience of a clear and specific measure of leadership.

The LRC training area had twenty "stations"—large enclosed areas separated by tall cinder-block walls. At each station, we were broken down into five- or six-man teams. Unlike our other exercises, no leader was formally designated. Instead, our team was briefed on a complex problem we had to solve in a given period of time. At one station, for example, our scenario and mission was to take a combat team across a deep, mined river (a ditch filled with muddy water) in order to bring desperately needed ammo to a unit on the other side. The tools we were given to accomplish this task were a few strands of rope, two short wooden planks (neither was long enough to bridge the ditch), and a heavy ammunition can, which represented the ammo we had to get to the other side.

NCOs stood atop the walls recording their observations on clipboards.

As I learned later, the mission—like most LRC missions—was just about impossible to accomplish, given the materials and time allotted. The aim was not to see who succeeded in completing the task but to see who took charge, how teams formed, and how well each of us contributed to the team effort to solve the problems. As mentioned, there was no chosen leader. There was no direction or guidance. The tasks to be done may have been doable, maybe not.

Team members shot out ideas. How do we process them? We can't process twenty ideas at once. How do we work the task? Do we tie the planks together? Anchor them down with some people, then cross with others? Anchor them down on the other side and let the rest cross? There was time pressure as well as the pressure of the problem itself.

It was not hard to motivate a bunch of Type A officer candidates to shout out instructions and try to take charge. It was more a matter of whom the team would *let* take charge or accept as the leader rather than who was willing to stand up and assume command. Since there was no preassigned rank, position, or seniority, as in other exercises, both the power and the authority to lead had to come from those being led. The problems were deliberately frustrating, and we had no idea how we were being evaluated. We had not been challenged in that way before; we had just put our shoulders into getting a demanding task done under the pressure of screaming NCOs who'd long since hammered into us not to question but to act. Here we had to question, form a team from scratch, and act without specific guidance; and we had to do all that under desperate time pressure.

That course fascinated me long after I had gone through it. As I've looked back on it and seen it later as an evaluator, I've realized how complex and rich it was in leadership lessons. The assumption of leadership with no clear authority to lead, the rapid building of a team, the ability to function as a team, difficult problem-solving processes, and the role of the led in an undefined and unstructured situation were but a few of the leadership challenges that I drew out of this experience.

Until then my leadership experience had consisted of simple exposure to impressive Marine leaders or assignments to lead where I went through the motions as best as a nineteen-year-old officer candidate could. This was the first experience that inspired me to look seriously at leadership in a much deeper way.

Since then, I've found my thinking about leadership lessons falling into two categories, each driven by an event I either directly experienced or witnessed.

The first is triggered by what I call a "leadership moment"—a striking act of positive or negative leadership that's worth noting as a lesson learned and dropping into my kit bag.

When I was a brand-new lieutenant platoon commander, for example, I paid careful attention to how my platoon sergeant, a decorated Korean War vet, masterfully read our young Marines. He knew exactly when to be the hard-nosed NCO disciplinarian and when to be a compassionate father figure. He seemed to know intuitively what approach was needed. After witnessing his deft handling of a situation, I would ask him how he made his read and determined his approach. I learned from his insights, which were based on his many years of experience.

The second category is triggered by events like the LRC, which have sparked me to think about leadership more broadly and deeply and to take a more philosophical approach to it. I was inspired to write this book because of such an event . . . or, I should say, series of events.

In 2006, on the book tour for *The Battle for Peace,* I repeatedly got a question from audiences that initially gave me pause and eventually forced me to consider my own presuppositions. In my talks, I would normally lay out the essence of the book—the seismic change that came after the collapse of the Cold War and the complex swarms of follow-on changes that I had been seeing from the frontlines. After the talk came questions from the audience.

"General," someone might ask, "we can relate to what you're saying about a changing world. We see it too. Does this mean there has to be a different way to lead in this different world?" Or perhaps: "If leaders are to be successful in this new world, must they adopt new ways to lead that significantly differ from those in the past?"

My response to these questions changed as I thought more about what my questioners were really asking and why.

"I really haven't given much thought to the issue of how leading has changed in this changing world," I answered initially. "Of course, leaders have to understand the changes and their impacts, but beyond that, it seems to me that the principles of good leadership are timeless and continue to apply."

But as the question kept coming from so many disparate audiences, I began to have doubts. These people are telling me something, not asking me something, I realized. They're out there in the trenches, where they're seeing failing or ineffective leadership, and they're wondering if this is just a bad patch of bad leaders or something more serious.

This realization caused me to move my thinking deeper and to look beyond the changing world and its consequences. I saw I also had to look hard at why leaders have succeeded or failed in the midst of all this change. Who was failing? Who was succeeding? Why?

My answers to these questions began to grow into the substance of this book.

IN MY THIRTY-NINE YEARS of service in the Marine Corps, I have led and been led in desperate combat, in tough and complicated crises, and in a wealth of other highly charged and difficult situations. I have known true leadership when its absence would have been catastrophic. I have taught leadership courses and, after retirement, consulted and lectured on leader development for businesses and other organizations. And I have personally witnessed many world leaders work through difficult decisions in war and in conflict resolution.

"What is leadership?" I've asked myself again and again. "What must a person do to become a true leader or to turn others into true leaders?"

Does knowing leadership personally, reflecting on it intellectually, and experiencing it intimately make leadership easy to understand?

No.

LEADERSHIP IS NOT MYSTERIOUS. At its core it is very simple: It is the ability to get people to do what we want them to do.

It's hard to argue with that statement, yet most of us intuitively feel that it's not enough. True leadership demands other essential qualities. To the core statement—"get people to do what we want them to do"—most of us would add something like:

1. In an ethical, moral, responsible way
2. That they enjoy, feel good about, and feel fulfilled in doing
3. That builds a cohesive and well-functioning team
4. That brings respect and admiration for the leader and the organization
5. That brings success to the enterprise

"Get people to do what we want them to do" focuses on the interaction of leading and following. It assumes leaders possess both authority and power over the led. The led acknowledge the leader's capacity to lead and allow the leader to direct and guide their actions. The first of the corollary elements points to the leader as the conscience of the organization. It focuses on the principles the leader should follow, the positive traits he should possess, and on his personal responsibility for the outcome of the act of leadership. Results flowing out of true leadership should be positive and not destructive. The second focuses on the effects on the led. It is hoped that in following a leader, the led will achieve pride, enjoyment, loyalty, and a sense of accomplishment. The third focuses on building a team, an organization that exceeds the sum of its parts because of the motivation, skill, and direction provided by the leader. The fourth focuses on the positive reaction the led, the leader's superiors, and all other stakeholders in the enterprise should feel toward the leader. The last focuses on a successful outcome. Leading that doesn't accomplish the mission, achieve the bottom line, or gain the objective in the most effective and efficient way is, after all, pointless. These elements are basic and timeless and can give us a good starting point for understanding leadership. It's impossible to imagine any responsible transaction involving leaders and led that doesn't include each of these elements as a foundation.

I'M HARDLY ALONE IN knowing true leadership when I see it. And I'm not alone in having experienced bad leadership. All of us have seen both good and bad and have a pretty clear idea why and how it went good or bad. Yet we still struggle to understand what we ourselves need to do in order to become good leaders or to turn others into good leaders. Future leaders, like the young Marines and university students I have taught, are searching for clear-cut rules and prescriptions for good leadership and for definitive processes that will make them good leaders.

The last century saw more significant thinking about leadership than in the past. Theories about it were generated; ways to make leaders were designed. We had passed into an era when assuming the divine right to lead was rapidly becoming unacceptable and the need to build leaders from the masses was critical. We started with the idea that a good person made a good leader, then evolved to a belief that we could educate good leaders. Later we came to realize that leaders are not all the same (there are many styles of leadership), and that power and authority come in more than one form. Along with these insights came the realization that leaders need evaluated experience if they are to develop fully. Each of these elements is necessary but the last is key.

BUILDING A GOOD PERSON

How are leaders made? What makes a truly superb leader? Can we predict who will become one? Can we develop programs to recruit,

educate, and train reasonably talented people and build them into future leaders? Or are leaders born and not made, and does leadership
simply come naturally to some and not to others?

These were big questions at the beginning of the twentieth century. After most of the world had rejected the concept that leadership passed by noble blood from father to son—or more rarely to
daughter—people now had to choose leaders and be in the business
of making them. During the last century, thousands of theories were
brought forth and promoted as answering the leadership question. I
have read countless analyses of great leaders and their common
qualities, all trying to answer this question.

For many years, it was thought that the essential nature of leadership could be determined scientifically and that this knowledge could
be translated into programs for selecting and training leaders, just as
we have programs to select and train pilots or doctors. The lives of superior leaders were studied and dissected to discover those special
qualities that made them great; programs were developed to transfer
these qualities over to those expected to become future leaders. You'd
put the raw human material into one end of the leader-making machine, and the process of character building and education would
produce leaders. It was like *Star Trek* teleporters, but with a bonus:
You come out better than you go in.

In the Marine Corps, as in the other services, this approach took a
somewhat different form. Since the military services obviously want
to build a strong, positive character in each of their leaders, we were
taught that the process of building an ideal leader first requires building an ideal *person*. As an aspiring Marine officer, I was exposed to
long lists of personal qualities, ideal traits, and guiding principles that
I was expected to develop and master. Quality leadership was reduced
to a scientifically determined foundation of eleven principles and
fourteen traits.

The principles were:

1. Know yourself and seek self-improvement.
2. Be technically and tactically proficient.

3. Develop a sense of responsibility among your subordinates.
4. Make sound and timely decisions.
5. Set the example.
6. Know your Marines and look out for their welfare.
7. Keep your Marines informed.
8. Seek responsibility and take responsibility for your actions.
9. Ensure assigned tasks are understood, supervised, and accomplished.
10. Train your Marines as a team.
11. Employ your command in accordance with its capabilities.

The traits were:

1. *Dependability.* The certainty of proper performance of duty.
2. *Bearing.* Creating a favorable impression in carriage, appearance, and personal conduct at all times.
3. *Courage.* The mental quality that recognizes fear of danger or criticism, but enables a man to proceed in the face of it with calmness and firmness.
4. *Decisiveness.* Ability to make decisions promptly and to announce them in a clear forceful manner.
5. *Endurance.* The mental and physical stamina measured by the ability to withstand pain, fatigue, stress, and hardship.
6. *Enthusiasm.* The display of sincere interest and exuberance in the performance of duty.
7. *Initiative.* Taking action in the absence of orders.
8. *Integrity.* Uprightness of character and soundness of moral principles; includes the qualities of truthfulness and honesty.
9. *Judgment.* The ability to weigh facts and possible solutions on which to base sound judgments.
10. *Justice.* Giving reward and punishment according to the merits of the case. The ability to administer a system of rewards and punishments impartially and consistently.
11. *Knowledge.* Understanding of a science or an art. The range of one's information, including professional knowledge and an understanding of your Marines.

12. *Tact.* The ability to deal with others without creating offense.
13. *Unselfishness.* Avoidance of providing for one's own comfort and personal advancement at the expense of others.
14. *Loyalty.* The quality of faithfulness to country, the Corps, the unit, to one's seniors, subordinates, and peers.

These principles and traits were printed on cards that we carried everywhere and memorized. If we mastered the principles and developed the traits, we would, in theory, be on our way to becoming the superb leaders the Corps wanted. We were tested and given assignments in order to visibly demonstrate these traits and principles. The Corps' fitness reports at every stage of our careers were structured to assess how well we demonstrated the traits and practiced the principles in leading our Marines. This evaluation played a large part in determining whether we were given greater responsibilities and promoted. I can remember countless counseling sessions by senior officers reviewing my fitness reports and assessing how well I exhibited, or didn't exhibit, those desired principles and traits. Blocks were checked in descending order assessing how well we demonstrated these principles and traits: outstanding, excellent, above average, average, below average, and unsatisfactory. I was told of my strengths and my weaknesses, and how to improve. I was judged as an individual according to how well I was perceived to have succeeded or failed to achieve mastery of the traits and principles.

As with most leader development programs with their origins in the early twentieth century, our system was based on learning how to become a perfect individual, then demonstrating that in leadership assignments. Build good character and you build a good leader.

In most leadership books written today by prominent leaders, academics, or self-help gurus, we see similar lists of qualities or principles. The secret to success lies in following the author's "Seven Ls of Leadership" or "Five Pillars of Successful Leadership."

It would be hard to argue with the theory. But something is missing.

Long ago I read an exhaustive analysis of history's great military leaders, written by a retired U.S. Army lieutenant colonel and historian, that started me doubting the utility of lists like these as the sole means of judging leadership. According to the study, the only common qualities among great leaders were courage, intellect, and a strong, determined will. This analysis made me realize that memorizing lists and trying to be the perfect person weren't enough to shape me into the leader I wanted to be or the Corps expected me to be. Learning leadership was more difficult and complex than that.

Building character and striving to be a good person are certainly good things. Anyone who mastered the lists and based his actions on them had to be a far better person than someone who didn't, but few of us reach leadership by following that path alone. We all know good people who are not good leaders. The human being who gets shoved into the leadership machine is not a lump of unformed clay. As humankind has learned over many millennia, ideal people with exceptional character traits are exceedingly rare. Sometimes truly good people fail as leaders, and sometimes deeply flawed people prove to be great ones.

I have no doubt that scientific studies can accurately reflect the reality of leadership; and I don't object to efforts to teach leadership techniques or to develop good people with desirable attributes, this training can enhance a leader's leadership skills, and we can certainly use more good people. Sixteen years of Catholic education and thirty-nine years in the Marine Corps have imprinted positive character traits that continue to make me, the nuns, and the drill sergeants proud.

But we must never forget that character development, leadership education, and technical training, however useful, are no substitutes for the real experience of leading. They will never by themselves create a leader who can make hard choices in tough, changing, or surprising conditions. Nor must we forget that humans are complex beings with an infinite range of personalities, temperaments, characteristics, capabilities, and styles of interpersonal interactions. Some of us are outgoing and gregarious; others are more reserved. Some of us are naturally open and curious; others focus on only a few strong interests. Some of us are tightly wound and driven; others are more relaxed. Some of us display natural wit or humor; others do not. Some of us exercise tact; others are blunt and frank. We are still not very successful at understanding what makes humans so different from one another and why and how they develop so uniquely. We are still too often surprised by who succeeds and who fails.

Leadership development that ignores this reality will inevitably fall short of its aims. You can't produce leaders in a cookie-cutter assembly line process that wants to radically alter human nature and produce ideal look-alike models. Neither can you create the perfect leader just by modeling the perfect person. Human beings are far too varied and complex for such simplistic methods.

TRAINING A GOOD LEADER

Memorizing lists was not all I learned from the Marine Corps about becoming a leader—far from it!

As a young, inexperienced lieutenant, I was assigned as an infantry "adviser" to the Vietnamese Marine Corps. That was in fact a misnomer; there wasn't much in the way of advice I could give the battle-hardened, small-unit leaders I dealt with each day. My primary contribution came from my ability to get them American firepower and other forms of support and coordination. Their contributions to my own development as a leader were far greater than anything I could give them. Over the course of my tour of duty, I observed more than thirty Vietnamese Marine officers leading in combat. Since each one bore the responsibility of command in the heat of the action, I was able to watch how they led under trying conditions . . . yet with some degree of detachment (although no one is really detached during a firefight).

I saw great differences in character, personality, and temperament and leadership styles and methods. All these officers were brave and competent; and the vast majority were successful leaders. Yet some led with great fire and animation while others were steady and cool. Some led from the front while others directed actions from more central positions. Some could process and coordinate complex battlefield activities simultaneously while others seemed to focus on them sequentially.

That year of personal observation of leadership under fire led me to conclude that there is no individual template for successful leadership. This conclusion was again confirmed when I later led an infantry company of U.S. Marines in Vietnam and saw similar diversity and similar success in my brother captains, in my lieutenants, and in my NCOs.

WE ALL COME WIRED with unique character and personality traits that we can change only with the greatest difficulty, if at all. Some traits will be assets, and some will be liabilities. Those that may be less than perfect need not hinder a leader's development. Potential leaders can work to recognize, appreciate, and understand these traits and to minimize their negative impact on their leadership role. Acting on their own special strengths, acknowledging their own limitations, leading in a style that best suits their own personalities, and emulating leaders that match up well with personalities like theirs are ways that people can be taught to develop their own leadership persona and style.

We mature as leaders and become a composite of our experiences, learning, and observation. I was a very different leader as a captain than I was as a lieutenant. The first years of leadership were trial and error and testing what I thought might work. I had to find my own leadership persona and learn how to connect to those I led.

Now and again, essential leadership qualities will come naturally to this or that individual, but the vast majority of quality leaders are made through training, education, motivation, experience—which includes careful analysis of experience—and continuous interaction with proven leaders. Leadership development programs that allow potential leaders to build their qualifications in consonance with their natural personalities work best. Trying to make someone into something he or she isn't doesn't work. This doesn't mean we can't help people overcome or work around shyness or lack of self-confidence or other personality traits that may interfere with effective leadership.

In fact, doing so is necessary in leader development. It does mean we can appreciate unique personalities and talents and shape them in individualized ways to get the best results.

My service as a Marine has given me a rich set of leadership experiences that molded my character and defined me as a person. I know my strengths and my limitations because I have tested them to the fullest. I have seen my own mortality enough times to give me a true sense of my own priorities and to know what I cherish in life. I have had my faith and beliefs tried to a degree that has strongly reinforced them.

Far more than any instruction or program, the powerful experiences I went through as a Marine and the examples of strong leadership and role models I encountered day to day are what forged me into a leader. The hard knocks of experience and the lessons from those experiences were the real school of leadership. We developed and grew. It wasn't lists of perfect traits or classroom theory that made us leaders, it was the experience of leading and being led under trying conditions and then reflecting on what that taught us.

LEADERSHIP STYLES

Leadership styles range from authoritarian, to micromanaging, to delegating, to participatory.

We've all run into authoritarian or micromanaging leaders. In authoritarian organizations, the leaders say and the led do. Leaders listen to the led only when it pleases them to do so.

Micromanagers shove their directing hand into every level of an operation. The micromanager assumes that he and only he knows how best to get every job done. He exhibits little to no trust in his subordinates.

Delegating is the reverse of micromanaging. Delegating leaders trust that their subordinates have expertise enough to get the job done (though good leaders will step in when necessary to teach and guide). Yet some who delegate carry it to the extreme, and delegation becomes a means to avoid responsibility and accountability.

Participatory leaders realize that knowledge is not limited to the top of the leadership pyramid; it's distributed in varying degrees and intensities throughout the organization. Participatory leaders recognize that they must tap into the wisdom, strength, and experience of the led.

Because the world has changed so much in recent years, and with it the nature of the led, a participatory style normally works best today. But not always. Success depends on the situation, the leader's personality, the nature of the enterprise, and the functions required. Participatory and delegating approaches require great trust and a common thread of intent so that everyone knows where they are going and why. Authoritarian and micromanaging approaches work best with more passive populations where there is little initiative, knowledge, or self-assertion.

A leader's styles can change. He may see the need to begin his tenure as an authoritarian, then change as his team and leadership evolve. He himself may change as he realizes he needs a different approach to be successful.

In professional team sports, old-school, drill-sergeant-style coaches and managers rarely win anymore. Today's professional players do not relate well to that style. Tom Coughlin, the coach of the 2008 Super Bowl–winning New York Giants, famously transformed himself from an overcontrolling, inflexible autocrat, much hated by his near-mutinous players, to a seeker of his players' cooperation through communication, participation, and compassion. His self-transformation paid off.

Autocratic coaching may work when players begin their careers as young athletes, just as it does with young military recruits in boot camp. The socialization of recruits normally requires an authoritarian, or boot camp, approach; but as they grow, mature, gain confidence, and become their own persons, that approach turns them off.

One of the positions I held after I retired from the Marine Corps was executive vice president of DynCorp, a very complex government services company that specialized in security, construction, logistics, maintenance, and other support services. There is no simple model for running such an enterprise successfully. Our knowledge requirements for each segment of the business, our intricate teaming processes that are required to execute projects, and our global operating environment (over sixty-five countries) made it impossible to maintain single, narrow lines of authority and decision making. We needed the full participation and involvement of scores of leaders and led for virtually every action. Nor was our enterprise an exception. Virtually all organizations are becoming too complex and involved for single, directive approaches to leading.

Leading a participatory enterprise is not easy. A participatory approach requires strong leaders, great trust, and more emphasis on developing and judging character and intellect than on hammering out a production line of identically formed people. Since leaders cannot be produced by prescriptive education processes, leadership development must be based on more direct interaction of leader and led and on the lessons from experience. We must constantly learn from what we have done or witnessed. We can't let ourselves move on from one experience to another without continuously reexamining what happened, what was done, why it was done, and how it could have been done better. Leadership experiences left unexamined are useless and wasted.

THE MILITARY DID NOT stand still in my day.

In response to the agonies of the late 1960s and early 1970s—the racial problems, the generational problems, drugs, and the culture wars—our leadership training began to look at the impact of race and diversity. On top of all that, a radically different kind of force was emerging from what I initially came into—all volunteers. Because we wanted our young officers to be sensitive to these new realities, we emphasized human relations training and getting in touch with obstacles such as built-in prejudices and stereotypes that might get in the way of good leadership. It was difficult for proud institutions like our military services to adapt to a new environment and set of circumstances. Not everyone accepted the need to change and adapt. And certainly the wise voices of experience cautioned care as we changed and discarded old ways of doing things. Many seasoned leaders wisely counseled coupling training in human relations and understanding with leader development. In their judgment, you couldn't separate the two.

The late 1980s, the fall of the Soviet Union, and the resulting seismic changes throughout the world brought another shift. Conflict today is much different from the wars our fathers fought. It is far more complicated and confusing. The military has come to realize that today's smarter, better-educated, more knowledgeable subordinates will execute better, contribute more, and grow into better leaders if they themselves are engaged in the decision-making process. Leadership in the military has become more participatory.

Because military organizations depend on clear, decisive directions that are precisely given and precisely followed, leading a participatory enterprise in the military is even harder than in other organizations. Marines, for example, still retain their legendary discipline but with a great deal more decision-making interaction between the leaders and the led. Marines now value the communication of intent from leader to led and the understanding of the "why" by subordinates rather than blind obedience.

The Marine Corps has also realized the value of experience in our service schools—more specifically, the value of drawing on experience to develop leaders. Officers rigorously analyze military campaigns, reexamine their own past experiences, and visit places like the floor of the New York Stock Exchange to observe up close a seemingly chaotic, high-pressure, rapid decision-making environment. Experience (either real or vicarious) registers more forcefully than study of theory or of past leadership examples alone.

When I was a lieutenant colonel, one of my assignments was as an instructor at the Marine Corps Command and Staff College, where we educated our majors. I came to this assignment from command of an infantry battalion. My division commander, Major General Dave Twomey, a tough and much-admired senior officer, transferred at the same time to head up our Education Center, where he oversaw the staff college and all the other schools at our Quantico, Virginia, base. It wasn't long before the grizzled old general summoned the faculty members to his office. He was unhappy with the way we were teaching our majors—with our very traditional, standardized curriculum, classes, and lectures—and he let us know that in the most forceful, bellowing terms. He wanted his majors to experience warfare, not classes. During the year they spent at the college, he wanted every major to go through vicariously, but realistically, eight or nine "campaigns," as the general put it. "That major," he growled, "should leave here exhausted from fighting those military campaigns and analyzing their lessons." This approach baffled most of the older faculty. They didn't get what he was saying, but I did. He knew from decades of leadership and combat experience what best formed leaders. He wanted to base the course on historical campaigns, on exercises (in the field or computer simulated) that reflected military campaigns, and on personal reflections on campaigns those majors had experienced (real or in training). Disjointed, lectured theory did not, in his mind, teach, shape, and develop these young majors into the kind of senior leaders the Corps required. It didn't have context or coherence. Experience, real or vicarious, and the skill to draw lessons from that experience, gave leader development its relevance. This was not the imperfect science of developing ideal individuals; it was the real art of making leaders.

THE POWER TO LEAD

In 1965, I received a commission as an officer. Because that commission had behind it the force of authority of our government and our constitution, it conferred on me a position of authority and a degree of power.

Did the mere exercise of that power to get people to do something make me a true leader?

Hardly.

Sure, it was sufficient for giving orders and compelling obedience. But my Corps and my country wanted more from me. That commission was merely a basis for my authority, a starting point for my development as a leader.

No one can lead without the authority to lead. That authority can come from a number of sources. It can be inherent in the position a leader holds or it can come from his skill, personality, or experience. It can come from events that thrust a leader into a visible role that highlights his abilities in critical times. It can come from the led: You get elected. You get picked by the tribe. It can be bestowed from some higher authority. It can come from the resources you control, such as money or property. It can come from birth or inheritance. It can come from your personal qualifications, competence, or charisma. It can come from physical force. It can come from your earning it.

In sports we often hear of "leaders in the locker room"—players who assume a leadership role on their own and become sources of motivation for teammates even though they don't have designated leadership positions, such as captain or coach. We also hear of players who fail to take on a leadership role that is assumed by their position, such as quarterback.

Whatever the basis of authority, it transfers to the leader the power to lead—to effect events. Though power and its sources are essential to leadership, and most of us have a rough and ready understanding of power, power itself is hard to describe or to measure. Leaders can share it or retain it. It can be almost limitless or severely limited. It can be strong at times and wane or disappear at other times. It can be given or taken. It can be shaped and focused—aimed. Or it can be dissipated—leaked. A leader's effectiveness is determined by how well he wields it.

Today, power can't be assumed. It must be earned and used wisely, or it is lost. Today's world is far more competitive than the world I grew up in, with far more transparency. It is far easier to recognize who is succeeding and who is not. Every week, we get a measure of the ups and downs of the president's performance—his approval ratings. The performance of the president's lieutenants are likewise under constant scrutiny; and pressure from negative judgments of their performance can force dismissal. Witness the exit from the last administration of Defense Secretary Rumsfeld and other top leaders, and the revolving door of sports coaches and managers who don't deliver quick success. Holding on to power is harder than it once was—much more tenuous and fragile—and transfers of power happen far more frequently. More stakeholders than ever have a say on a leader's tenure.

After I received my commission, I was not expected to rest there. In my growth as an officer, I was expected to develop the power to lead beyond what my commission provided. I was expected to earn that power in positive ways, to never abuse it, and to wield it wisely . . . an impossible task unless I understood the power available to me at any given moment: its limits, its possibilities. I had to know how I could shape it, focus it, or restrain it. I had to be deeply aware of what I could and could not get done at any given moment.

No leader can be successful unless he truly understands the power he possesses, its sources, its limitations, and its potential to grow. A leader who does not understand his power can easily lose it. The old system of absolute and unchallenged power, once common in virtually every endeavor, rarely exists in today's world.

THE COMPLETE LEADER

The United States Army has described its leader development process as Be-Know-Do. This process is a progressive blend of character building (Be), education (Know), and experience (Do). It recognizes that leaders develop over time. They don't leave the womb ready to take charge. Nor is there a moment when they have achieved the fullness of leadership. It is a continuous learning process, in which "Do"—experience—is the heart of the process. This is what General Twomey was pressing us to understand.

But it's not just the experience that counts; it's what you draw out of it. I still draw on lessons from my Vietnam experiences over forty years later. But the richer context I have now gives me a far better framework for analyzing those experiences and appreciating their lessons than I had then. Times change, people change, and leaders and their understanding of leadership must change with them.

Their changing understanding of leadership will contain elements of both science and art.

The scientific understanding of leadership emphasizes the qualities that distinguish great leaders from others. The art of leadership emphasizes experiential learning and the participatory approach in which leaders draw on the talents and skills of all members of the enterprise yet retain the authority to lead.

What do we really know about today's good leaders? From my observations, I have learned that those who grow into superb leaders develop faster and in more complete ways than those who do not. They are adaptive leaders. They mature, relate, draw lessons from experiences, and sense their environment much more keenly. They possess an intellect, a sense of dogged determination and will, a charismatic nature, and a degree of personal courage above the norm. They are risk takers. They are passionate and enthusiastic. Their self-confidence and honesty inspire others.

These qualities are certainly not new. And though in today's complex world they are essential, they are still not enough to achieve success.

Even in the past, they were often not enough. The most successful leaders achieved their success not only because of personal qualities such as these, but because they could interact with and master their environment in ways lesser leaders could not. They were not statues on pedestals. They engaged dynamically with their world. They got dirty. They understood their times and possessed, adapted, or developed the traits and skills that best fit those times. In changing and confusing times, they could see and seize opportunities when others only saw challenges, obstacles, and risks.

Up until our own changed, changing, and confusing times, adaptive leaders have been rare. Today they are *necessarily* emerging . . . and in ever greater numbers. These new leaders sense the changes that are rapidly altering the face of the world, recognize the need to adapt to them, and are driving the organizations they lead toward successes old-style leaders can only envy. It's not enough, as it was in the past, to have just a few dynamic leaders at the top. The quality of adaptive leadership has to pervade the participatory organization that is becoming the successful model for today's environment. Any leader who fails to master this adaptability risks seeing his enterprise left in the dust.

In 1994, the Commandant of the Marine Corps, General Carl Mundy, gathered our senior generals (I was a lieutenant general at the time) at Camp Pendleton, California, for the first of several sessions to discuss the future of the Corps. He sensed we were in a new era with a rapidly changing world engulfing us. We needed to examine our role in this dynamic environment and ensure we were best prepared for the future. He had the additional insight that we senior leaders with decades of experience might bring a downside to these tasks: traditional thinking rather than the out-of-the-box approaches that were needed to adapt to a new world order.

In order to shake us up, he brought in a team of futurists—scenario builders of possible worlds. The scenarios they threw at us were truly creative, aimed at jolting us out of narrow, past-based thinking and at stretching our approaches and challenging our assumptions. In one scenario, we had to defend the earth from an invasion by aliens from outer space. It got a good laugh. But it also forced our thinking beyond the old paradigms that bound us. Other scenarios were less outlandish but no less provocative.

We got it. General Mundy's jolt worked.

Addressing the role, structure, missions, and relevance of our institution in a rapidly and profoundly changing world required innovative and unbounded thinking. We needed to break the framework that defined our comfort zone if we were going to be able to offer truly innovative concepts and ideas. In the process, we learned a lot about ourselves and about our institution.

Timeless qualities of leadership will remain timeless. But today's successful leaders have molded these timeless qualities to the changed environment we now face and have developed necessary new qualities that characterize new leaders and new organizations.

BUILDING A GOOD TEAM

Good leaders cannot claim success unless they can build good organizations. The people in these organizations, in the current environment, need to be fused with qualities such as adaptability, innovation, vision, and all the other leadership attributes that used to come from the top down but now must run in all directions in the enterprise. In other words, a few successful individual leaders in charge aren't enough. They must build a culture of leadership that becomes the identity of the organization rather than just that of the top leaders.

One of my fitness report counseling sessions as a senior captain company commander was different from any I had previously experienced. We had ten captains in our battalion, and our rating scheme encouraged the reporting senior to rank us in order. We captains knew that the battalion commander had a favorite. (I'll call him Bill.) Our CO made no bones about it; he openly admired and praised him. (We, Bill's peers, did not hold him in such regard.) On one typical occasion, I was standing next to the CO as he turned his gaze on Bill: "Ah," he said with a big fatherly smile, "he reminds me so much of myself when I was his age."

The rest of us stoically accepted our inevitable fate on the upcoming fitness reports.

When I entered the CO's office for my turn for counseling, he brusquely handed me my fitness report. "Read it," he ordered.

I did; then my jaw dropped. I was rated number one.

I guess my shock was clearly evident.

"What's the matter?" the CO asked.

"Well, sir, frankly, I thought that since you have been so open in praising Bill, he would be number one. . . . Not that I'm complaining!"

"Read Section C," he told me.

Section C was where reporting seniors added their own remarks.

His were short, terse bullets laying out the accomplishments of my company. Such as "Led battalion in reenlistments. . . . Scored highest in the Tactical Test."

"Look," the CO said, "I like Bill. He is a great individual leader, probably the best in the battalion, in my opinion, but your company was superior. My judgment is based on performance of the organization you lead. Whatever you're doing works."

That was for me one of my greatest "leadership moments." It was the first time I was judged primarily on the performance of my unit and not on how a senior subjectively rated my own individual qualities. It made sense. I certainly liked the outcome!

But as I thought more about it, I realized how rarely we judge the effect of a leader on his organization. How often do we judge leadership on how well our organization performs? In the military, we often talk about the "halo effect" that occurs when an individual's appealing traits or reputation give him a leg up before he has to prove himself. His appearance, previous personal awards, education credentials, articulate manner, or other qualities position him ahead of the rest of the pack. Even if his unit is not as good as others, he still gets the highest ranking or promotion.

We often pay extraordinary compensation packages to CEOs based on these kinds of factors. And then all too often, they run lousy organizations.

We can't separate the individual leader from the performance of the organization and then make excuses for his failure, as if his leadership has meaning outside his organization. It's fine to build a good person and a good leader, but the complete leadership package comes only when we build a good organization. You cannot separate the two. Leadership today must fuse individual character, ability to lead, and the performance of the organization. Checking only one or two of these blocks is not enough.

THE NEW LEADER

Those nagging questions from my book tour triggered my realization that good character alone is no longer enough to define a good leader; that successful leaders today are being trained with ever greater emphasis on experiential development; and that there must be greater emphasis on a leader's ability to build an interactive leadership organization rather than one based on top-down individual leadership skill. In today's world, we need to create enterprises that function effectively throughout all their many dimensions yet work as a single organic whole. The hallmark of today's successful new leader is the ability to create and instill this culture of leadership, to build a leadership organization as opposed to an organization that is led.

Can we determine the qualities today's leaders must possess if they are going to achieve these goals? I looked hard and have come up with some that stand out.

From my observations, eleven new or newly molded qualities are the core elements modern leaders need if they are going to create a culture of leadership and be successful in today's challenging world:

1. The new leader has to have a clear and confident understanding of himself and how to keep himself performing as a leader in this dynamic environment.
2. The new leader has to possess a strong ethical sense. He is the conscience of the organization, and his conscience shapes the ethical behavior of the entire organization.
3. The new leader must listen to, understand, and relate to the new led and to what it takes to make them productive, fulfilled, and motivated.
4. The new leader has to understand the environment he and his organization must operate within. The leader and his organization must be learning entities that constantly take the pulse of the dynamic, complex, and ever-changing environment swirling about them.
5. The new leader must understand his or her organization to its roots yet be able to function with little or no structure and to change and morph structures as the environment demands. Today's leader cannot be a slave to the organization. It cannot control him. He must control it.

6. The new leader needs to be able to operate at a blisteringly fast pace and be quick to harness ever evolving technologies. This over-heated new world changes ever faster. A technology can be obsolete almost immediately after it's developed. Cautious delay is no longer wise or prudent.

7. The new leader has to be far more curious, broadly knowledgeable, and widely educated than leaders of the past. This curiosity springs from an innate desire to totally understand today's world. Without such curiosity, few leaders can function in modern endeavors and situations.

8. The new leader must communicate clearly and articulately with his organization and with the larger public. He can no longer be the faceless top of a chain of command.

9. The new leader has to develop different—and stronger—decision-making skills than his predecessors. Honed intuition, rapid recognition of swiftly developing patterns and trends, quick input processing, and clear communication of his directions and intent are all hallmarks of this new, more decisive leader.

10. The new leader must be able to lead in times of crisis and change. Today, organizations are exposed to more crisis-generating events and dynamic shifts of ever greater severity than ever before. A leader's ability to calmly steer a course through these confused seas has become critical to the survival of any enterprise.

11. The new leader must think and act strategically. He must plot the organization's future course and guide it to achieving the vision he has clearly articulated. He must be able to hold fast to his vision even as he responds and adapts it to a changing world. At a time when vision has become more vitally necessary to survive and prosper than ever, remarkably few leaders possess this critical skill.

Each of these eleven core elements forms the subject of a chapter.

The best-of-breed successful leaders I have seen emerging in this challenging new world combine these elements with the tried-and-true qualities that have proven successful in the past. That fusion of the tried and true with the innovative and adaptive is the key.

FOUR

SELF-KNOWLEDGE

"If you know the enemy and know yourself," wrote Sun Tzu, "you will win a hundred battles."

Sun Tzu may have been thinking in a purely military context, and his words can certainly be interpreted to relate primarily to such factors as knowing your combat power relative to your adversary's. But in my view, he had more than that in mind; he was encouraging the leader to make a reflective, personal assessment of his character, his strengths, and his limitations.

You're probably reading this book because you are interested in leadership and striving to improve your own leadership skills. Sun Tzu's words apply to you as you face that task no less than they apply to the combat commander facing battles.

WHO ARE YOU?

I have facilitated numerous leadership sessions in the military, government agencies, business organizations, academic institutions, and other enterprises. I like to begin these sessions by asking each participant to write down answers to several questions. Questions such as:

- Who are you?
- What defines you?

- What values are most important to you?
- Do you live your values?
- What do you see is your life's purpose?
- What will you die for?

When I ask that first question, Who are you? I lead the participants to believe that their answers will be collected or that I may call on them to present their answers to the group. I offer the participants no guidance, nor do I answer any questions regarding the task. "Just tell me, in any manner you wish, who you are." You can imagine the looks I get.

After they finish, I don't collect their answers, nor do I ask participants to disclose them. Their replies, I tell them, are for their own consideration.

Next I ask them to reconsider and revise their answers. And I rephrase the initial question from Who are you? to Who am I? I do this because their initial answers to Who are you? are invariably aimed at impressing others in case they are called on or their answers are collected. They're trying to sell themselves to somebody, to present their résumé. But when they answer Who am I? they know I'm not going to see or collect their answers. And they begin to realize that they are defining themselves to someone else in a different way from how they are defining themselves to themselves.

I want them to see how their honest and private answers can differ from their public ones. They all quickly realize that they have rarely, if ever, looked into this mirror so deliberately.

After I gave this assignment to one of my college classes, a visibly upset young student asked to see me afterward.

"What's upsetting you?" I asked.

"My answers to the first part were pure bullshit," he answered.

I told him not to get too worked up about it. "As you could see from the reactions in class, most of the other students felt pretty much the same way."

"Yeah," he said, "but I thought I was better than that."

He learned something about himself. That was the purpose of the exercise.

Once they have bared their souls (at least to themselves), we discuss several possible ways these questions could have been answered and what those different answers might say about a person's character, ambitions, and personal values. "In the first part, where you are presenting your image to the outside world," I ask, "did you describe yourself by your occupation, status, values, family? What does that say about you? What changed in the second part, and why?" Now, certainly I'm no psychologist, and I do not intend to turn these drills into psychoanalytic sessions. I just use them to spur genuine introspection.

It's a fascinating drill.

Things get really interesting as our sessions continue and participants begin to realize that their initial sense of who they are is usually not very well thought out. Few people have spent much time thinking about who they are. And most are surprised to recognize that they haven't done this before. Young people are especially uneasy at the realization that they are developing an "outside me" and an "inside me"; older people tend to be more defensive and in greater denial. The older ones are generally less willing to acknowledge that they gave different answers to the first part than the second part.

In my opinion, any consideration of leadership should begin with this kind of self-assessment . . . a truth that I'm not the first to discover. Many organizations open leadership training sessions with personality tests and other kinds of formal self-discovery. It's become popular for companies and other organizations to give Myers-Briggs personality tests or executive assessment tests. These tests can obviously be useful for both individuals and organizations; but too often I've seen them become tools for organizations to evaluate leadership potential rather than a means for individuals to gain better insights into themselves. Organizations seek a particular leadership "profile" in the mistaken belief that it will predict leadership success.

Why is knowing yourself important?

Today's world has become high pressure and demanding for leaders. The rules and codes leaders must lay down and enforce are becoming less clear and accepted. The demand for more personal interaction with those they lead adds to the pressure. Modern leaders in all walks of life are called on to make significant sacrifices. These high-pressure demands create a hard mistress who robs leaders of the parts of their being that keep them balanced. Workaholic leaders can drive themselves, their people, and their organizations into the ground. Leaders have to pick their fights, know when to "surge," and constantly take their own temperature so that they don't suffer the all-too-common burnout that plagues so many organizations and their leaders.

Achieving these goals requires a strong, well-developed character based on a solid set of values, a strong moral code that is lived day-to-day, and a clear philosophy of leadership that the leader can share with his team. Leaders have to establish these qualities in their own mind and make them clear to those they lead and answer to by their actions and behavior. You can't begin to articulate this set of values, this code, and this philosophy until you understand who you are and what you want to be—and to stand for—as a leader. You don't want to evolve into a one-dimensional person. Early on leaders have to commit to being a complete person. The first step on that path is to understand how you've been formed.

PERSONAL CODES AND CORE VALUES

In the past, we relied on institutions, such as family, church, and school, to instill a personal moral code in young adults, who then went charging into the world on their own. That code provided a foundation and guidance on values, worth, and character.

Today, unfortunately, these institutions can no longer be counted on to provide a reliable moral foundation. This truth was first pointed out to me some years ago by a friend who ran our Marine recruit training. His words have stuck with me. "Dysfunctional families, less relevant religious institutions, and poor schools are no longer shaping young people as they once did," he explained. "Increasingly we in the military have to take on that task." That is a sad commentary on our society.

In the future, organizations like the military, colleges and universities, and employers may be required to shape us as moral persons in the void left by the decreased moral presence of families, churches, and lower schools.

"On what foundation can we build our personal code in these confusing times? Are there universal values? Can we identify all-encompassing and unfailing anchors and guides for our actions?"

When I pose this question in my university classes, the immediate reaction is "Yes, of course!"

Yet, in every case, as students offer candidates for universal status, other students identify exceptions.

Somebody will always propose life as a universal value. How can you get more basic than that? Without life we have nothing.

And yet my students will invariably find exceptions even to that primal reality and debate the right to choose versus the right to life or the morality of the death penalty. Others debate cultural differences in views on the value of life: "We call them suicide bombers; others call them martyrs."

Freedom and democracy. Ultimate truth. Justice. The Golden Rule. Jesus' Beatitudes. You name it; and you'll get an argument over its universality . . . or at least over its universal acceptance. Multinational corporations I've worked with have difficulty with this issue as they work toward establishing global codes of conduct for employees from disparate cultures.

I like to approach this area from a different direction. I like to emphasize with my students that their job as ethical people is not to search for the possible chimera of universal values that they can then blindly follow. Their job is to find and state for themselves strong core values that they will faithfully practice.

By definition, core values should be foundational and few. They are the bedrock of what defines your value code. For me, core values include integrity, honor, and honesty. As a man and a leader, I try to inform all my decisions and actions with these values. I simply cannot operate in a way that goes counter to them. In my eyes, doing that would make me less than human. How can I know if I'm being untrue to myself if I don't know who I am or want to be?

If, as I believe, the best way to define yourself is through the core values you believe in and try to live up to, then it's worth looking at some core values.

THE BLESSING OF INTEGRITY

I believe we have an obligation to speak and seek the truth in everything we do. To do less is cowardly. A person lies, cheats, or steals only out of fear, incompetence, or lack of self-worth. Today's society makes excuses for these flaws. We "spin" instead of lie. We blame others for our faults—parents, teachers, coaches, the press, the system. We cover up mistakes. It is rare to see someone stand on principle and take responsibility for his actions, and it is even rarer to see that person rewarded. It's much more common to see those who fail be forgiven without significant consequence. Where are the heroes? In every recent leadership failure, there have been no heroes. We need them today—leaders who don't play by the compromising "rules" of politics, business, or personal behavior that mark our modern society.

THE CURSE OF LOYALTY

Many of us have the mistaken view that loyalty to a person or organization is a high core value—perhaps the highest core value. In a conflict over other values, even with integrity, loyalty must prevail. To be disloyal, it is thought, is to commit the ultimate sin.

In organizations throughout history, leaders have demanded blind loyalty ahead of all other values. In return for loyalty, they provided security and order.

Security, order, loyalty . . . each of these is essential to the smooth running of an organization or of a society; but none of them is a core value.

The George W. Bush administration was famous for demanding unfailing loyalty—if you were a member of the team, no matter what you were asked to do, you owed blind loyalty to the team.

No!

If you ask people for loyalty, you owe them integrity and honesty in return. You don't just owe them loyalty. Loyalty itself does not ensure honesty, credibility, competence, or ethical performance. If you don't find these qualities in your leaders, how can you be loyal to them? How can you be loyal to lies or corrupt practices? Or even to spin?

A leader I once knew had only one thing on his desk, a sign that said "Integrity." He compromised it with every heartbeat. This hypocrisy created a tremendously negative work environment and lack of trust that permeated the entire organization.

If your organization is engaged in shoddy business practices, and if its success depends on unethical behavior and loyal followers who accept these things, your loyalty is worse than worthless. It's nothing but calculated self-interest that will fall apart the moment self-interest gets pushed in another direction. These organizations may work for a time in today's world; but not for long. At some point, the "loyal" followers will always rat on each other or someone's conscience will win out, and the system will fall apart.

Loyalty in and of itself is not a core value. It must always be a value secondary to integrity and honesty. The whistleblower who stands on principle should be honored and valued far more than the individual who remains blindly loyal in the face of immoral, unethical, or criminal behavior. Too often the *merely* loyal get respect and rewards while the honorable whistleblower gets cast out into the darkness.

That's the flaw in the idea that if you're disloyal, you've committed the ultimate sin. *No.* If you're dishonest and you lack integrity, you've committed the ultimate sin. Loyalty can't stand on its own.

From integrity, honor, and honesty, loyalty will follow, as will many other values, such as trust. But you can't say "My principle core value is loyalty to the leadership and the institution."

A variation on this theme comes up when an institution's leadership chooses to protect the institution before protecting its people or principles.

The best recent example of this is of course the response of the Catholic Church to sexual abuses by Catholic clergy. Criminal priests were shielded by the hierarchy and their crimes were covered up, while the young men and women who suffered abuses at their hands were ignored, shunted aside, or demonized.

How should a good Catholic respond to these evils?

I'm a practicing Catholic. I love my faith and my church.

My priests expect me to be loyal to the church, to adhere to its tenets, to trust and respect the clergy. But how can I do that when the leadership has let me down by their lack of integrity? The senior clergy talk about being open and honest about our sins and our sense of accountability for them, and then a significant part of that leadership structure belied both honesty and accountability when priests, and in particular cardinals and bishops, covered up the acts of the priest criminals and failed to protect the innocent faithful these priests have harmed. That part of the church's leadership has lost their right to my loyalty. They have betrayed the thousands of good and honorable clergy who have lived the life they committed to and who still have my loyalty.

I have been blessed to know good priests and nuns who shaped my life, faith, and character. My anger toward those priests or nuns who violated their vows has grown, though I have not encountered any myself. They have cast suspicion and doubt on the many devout men and women of the cloth who have served with honor. Worse yet, church leadership didn't act to deal with these violators in a manner expected by us or by the values the church has preached for two thousand years.

If church leaders can't offer us integrity, commitment, and honor, where can we anchor our loyalty? Remember, these people claim to act from higher standards than the rest of us.

A once-good organization has developed glaring flaws. It has not adjusted to the world we now live in. It has failed to understand the people who, with all their heart, desire to be faithful members. It has failed to answer the people's questions and needs. It's become an institution that serves itself. The organization has been valued more than the people . . . who are the very essence of the church. It has lost its direction because it has lost its sense of honor and integrity and a sense of who and what it is. I want my church to be relevant and respected by the next generations—by my children and grandchildren. The church will lose them if its leaders don't connect. I hope and pray that they have reflected and learned from their lack of appropriate leadership.

MILITARY UNITS ALL PRIZE loyalty, and they must—loyalty to your unit, loyalty to your buddy. But even here, loyalty does not prevail over integrity and honor.

After the atrocities were committed at Abu Ghraib, the young soldier who stood up and blew the whistle on those crimes was isolated and rejected. He became the bad guy—not those who committed the atrocities—because "he betrayed his unit." No! He was taught a set of principles. He was taught a code. He was taught to be honest. He was taught the difference between right and wrong. He was taught to shine a light on evils that he witnessed. He wasn't the one who betrayed his unit; those who committed the atrocities were.

Studies of people in combat have found that the biggest driver of posttraumatic stress disorder is some deep challenge that conflicts with a person's moral code, belief system, or sense of ethics. These ideals are naturally challenged in the brutality of combat. But if the leadership doesn't continually reaffirm those principles and the necessary honor and integrity that must exist even on the battlefield, what's acceptable and not acceptable—as when senior leadership becomes ever more vague and nuanced in their approach to torture—the people doing the fighting may find themselves facing agonizing choices that they can't handle. Losing your moral compass and compromising on your principles, what you stand for, what defines your society, and what you—man or woman—have been brought up to believe, affects you as forcefully as the death and destruction around you.

A PHILOSOPHY OF LEADERSHIP

In our schools for officers and enlisted leaders, we ask Marines to write a paper on their own personal philosophy of command. The purpose is to encourage them to reflect on and articulate their personal code for leading . . . and for living. I often ask students in my university classes and other leadership courses to do something similar.

You will never know if your personal code is challenged or compromised if you don't have one. Though your code will almost certainly evolve as you face particular demands and challenges, it's never too early to establish a base. The exercise in writing a leadership or command philosophy is designed to help leaders and aspiring leaders explore and reflect on their own beliefs, values, experiences, character, and approaches.

The goal I try to set for my students is not to be negatively self-critical. This is not the time for them to judge how they have screwed up. I simply ask them to ask themselves: How am I doing? Am I getting where I want to be? Am I making progress toward being the person and leader I want to be? Am I drifting away from my code?

Honesty with yourself allows you to develop in a positive way and to stay on course with your values and beliefs. There is no set format for the philosophy paper, but I ask students to describe how they have developed as leaders (what created their values, principles, and beliefs); what they've learned from their leadership experiences or studies; what expectations they have from those they lead; what goals, core values, and objectives they set for their organization; and what they expect of themselves (and what subordinates should expect of them).

It's not easy to work out your philosophy for the first time, but once you've done it, updating and evolving it becomes easier. I always urge my students to make a lifetime habit of taking their own pulse and checking themselves.

Many former students have told me how they continue to rework and refresh their philosophy every year or two or when they change positions. Their fundamental principles or values remain unchanged, they usually explain, but their growing fund of experiences and learning enhances their principles and allows them to articulate their philosophy much more clearly. Reworking their philosophy also becomes a self-check to ensure they are not drifting away from their code. It's an opportunity to take stock of themselves in their work life and their personal life.

THE CALLING

Leadership has become exponentially more difficult as the complexity of our world has increased. Values, principles, and rules that seemed rock solid a few decades ago are being challenged. Never has the need for inspirational leadership been greater. We need and want real heroes and leaders we can respect and admire, and those of us aspiring to fill that role have to be sure we measure up. We begin by asking ourselves why we want to lead and what motivates us to seek a leadership role.

Successful people are naturally ambitious. Without ambition, it's hard to imagine where motivation to grow and to lead would come from. But overambition is counterproductive; it can even be destructive. It alienates our coworkers and colleagues, sparks questions about our trustworthiness and objectives, and prevents us from acquiring the balance and social skills a leader must have. I have seen several exceptionally talented individuals destroy promising careers through their obsessive and excessive ambition. It seemed to be a sickness that they could not control. Everything was a competition and everyone a competitor. They manipulated and plotted to get ahead. They maneuvered for advantage. They schemed to sabotage their competitors. The tragedy was that they didn't need to do those things. Their talent and skills ensured success. But their acts of blatant ambition threw it away.

It is interesting to hear how people express their ambition. I have always been more impressed by those who express it in terms of increased responsibility rather than position. The young officer who tells me he wants someday to take on the challenge of commanding a division has my respect more than one who tells me he wants someday to be a general.

HOW DOES OUR WORK motivate us?

What we do for a living can be seen as a job, a profession, or a calling. A *job* is simply a means to an end. People who see their work as nothing more than a job simply use employment to gain the resources necessary to fulfill other needs or desires. They go through the motions. A *profession* goes much further: It has a code, requirement for entry, obligations, and a sense of accomplishment. It gives us credibility and stature because of its demands and value to society. A *calling* is true dedication of your life to a purpose at the sacrifice of almost all else.

I don't use these terms in this conventional way—in the sense that the individual's position determines which of these categories he falls into or uses to describe his work. I like to use them as descriptions of an attitude toward your life's work. All of us have come across service workers such as waiters who take their work as no less a profession or calling than an accomplished lawyer or a devoted religious cleric. And I have met lawyers and clerics who approach their work as a mere job. We have all marveled at the pride, enthusiasm, dedication, and commitment of people in the most humble jobs and at the lack of pride and commitment by some in more prestigious positions.

Today, far more than in the past, most of us who seek to lead want our work to be a calling to live a life that matters to us—a life that brings a sense of achievement and fulfillment and positively affects the lives of others. Few of us are satisfied to be identified only by our job description. We want far more than a leadership position that provides a reasonably secure and comfortable life. We want to know what our leadership means. We want our leadership to contribute to society. We want to grow in it, and we want it to grow because of us. We want our life's work to have a legacy of significance.

Most organizations have recognized this change and have acted to give their people the kind of identity that reflects this desire. Organizations have upgraded titles to enhance dignity, pride, and responsibility. We no longer see salesmen; it's now "sales associates." Car mechanics are now "automotive technicians." Every person employed by a bank now seems to be an "officer." This may seem like feel-good title inflation, but I think there's more to it than that. In many cases, it's a genuine acknowledgment of real performance and truly enhanced qualification. Cars are far more complex than they used to be. Mechanics need far more skills than they used to have. If we now require and demand more from our people, especially those who lead, then we should recognize their responsibilities and acknowledge their performance.

PERSPECTIVE POINTS

Our fast-paced, chaotic world puts unprecedented stress on modern leaders. Demands and pressures hit them from every direction: the scope and burden of their responsibilities, the constant pressure to perform at the top of their game, the often worldwide consequences of their decisions, the public visibility, and the personal and professional scrutiny.

All of these—and more—threaten to wear today's leaders down.

How does a leader steer a steady course through these reefs and shoals? How does he keep intact his balance, perspective, and personal well-being?

My personal solution is to get in touch with what I call "perspective points"—points in our lives when we *successfully* weathered crises, unpredictable challenges, traumatic events, or catastrophic losses: the death of a loved one, a serious injury or illness, the collapse of major plans or hopes, or the failure of a critical undertaking.

Getting through any big crisis is, by definition, difficult. But previous success proves that we can do it. *Because we did it!* Reflecting on our successful navigation through trying events gives us perspective on our current situation that we might not otherwise have; it allows us to realize that we have the strength and resilience to get through tough times.

One of my personal perspective points comes out of the war in Vietnam. On November 3, 1970, I was severely wounded on a remote hilltop near Danang. The emotions generated by my injury, the thoughts about my chances of survival, the injuries to the Marines in my command, the desperate fight to capture the hill, the subsequent trauma of recovery, and my lifelong thoughts and reflections on the experience have given me a lens through which I can view in their true light trying moments that have hit me later. Knowing I have been through worse than anything that can be thrown at me has given me the serenity and confidence in my abilities to get through today's trials.

It also gives me a greater appreciation for other elements of my life that give me balance. I now have a far greater appreciation of the creative and reflective time I can carve out of the hectic demands of life and leadership. I know how important it is to protect that time. I also have a far greater recognition of what I can control and what I cannot. I know how important it is to be able to let go. And I have greater appreciation for things outside my work: family, friends, and personal interests.

When I see someone who's been through a tough demoralizing experience, I always try to help him get it in perspective and look to the future. As he wrestles with problems that he will invariably see as far more devastating and unsolvable than they are, he needs a trusted outside voice that helps him deal with his troubles in a clear and rational way. It's always tough to do this on your own. We all need leaders, mentors, and friends who can help us through trying times and provide the clear perspective we are incapable of seeing from inside the turmoil of our problems.

PERSONAL CHANGE

"How much can a person change?" one of my college students asked me.

"Real change is not easy, but it can be done," I answered. "It's a matter of will, values, and the degree of commitment you are willing to make."

I tell future leaders whom I coach or instruct that we are on a "leadership journey." We need to stop periodically along the way and get our bearings, to make sure we are on course to achieve our goals. If we wait too long between the stops, it's harder to adjust or change. We get too set in our ways.

Have you ever tried to lose weight, stop smoking, or work out more? If you have, you know how hard it is to drum up the will and determination to see it through. It's even harder to change our more deep-set attitudes and become, for example, more patient, positive, encouraging, or considerate.

Personal development is one of the most significant attributes of a truly successful leader. If I had to pick a single indicator of a future top leader, I would say it's the degree of his commitment and determination to improve himself, on his own. Self-education, overcoming negative habits, improving professional skills, dealing with personal issues, managing time, balancing life's demands, ensuring his own well-being, improving self-discipline, and all the other things that are tough to do, easy to put off, and easy to compromise are exactly the things that mark a great leader today. Too many people with great potential want it done for them or to them. They make excuses for a few "flaws." That won't get them where they want to go.

How do you get there?

First, you have to get in touch with yourself. Then you need to decide who you want to be. Then you need to make the commitment to get there. And last, you must have a degree of honesty with yourself, clear vision about your personal goals, and sheer, painful determination.

FIVE

ETHICS

Warfare was once upon a time relatively simple: Classical conflicts between nation-states had long been codified, with agreed-on rules and conventions. Victory came by defeating the other side on the battlefield: Defeat the enemy's force and you win. In that context, a military leader could direct most of his attention and efforts to the military capabilities of the other side. "How must I set up, equip, and utilize my armed forces in such a way that I defeat his? How do I generate the preponderance of combat power and direct that at a critical time and place?"

Simplicity no longer holds. In recent times, conflict has radically changed. A military leader today is probably fighting a shadowy, elusive enemy. His focus now is not just on an opposing country's military forces but also on its people. He can no longer simply generate the preponderance of combat power. Success requires generating international legitimacy, relevance to the population, simultaneous reconstruction of societies, and moral force.

Now a military leader may have to choose to take a risk and restrain his use of military force in ways that may handicap his combat power, not only because taking that action is morally right *but* because it may also gain for him an overwhelming advantage in moral authority that, in the long term, may be more valuable in accomplishing the mission than combat power.

It's a risk. A tough ethical choice: Is losing the combat edge a price worth paying if you gain the support of the people? What happens when that choice may bring greater harm to your own force?

Complex, multidimensional ethical choices are not the exclusive province of military leaders. Business leaders, political leaders, diplomats, and others face similarly tough choices.

One of my first encounters with this kind of complex, risky, moral choice came in Vietnam: I was a lieutenant then, and an adviser with a company of Vietnamese Marines, the only American assigned to the unit.

Our base camp was on one side of a hill, which we shared with a U.S. Army artillery battery commanded by a U.S. Army captain, who had set up on the other side of the hill in a Vietnamese cemetery. Because we shared the hill, the battery commander and I talked a lot.

One day the Vietnamese company commander came up to me with a worried expression on his face. "I just left a group of local village elders," he said. "Their cemetery is very important to them; and they're deeply concerned—really troubled—that they don't know what's going on there. They're worried that the artillery battery will desecrate or destroy the graves, and it's really upsetting them and the villagers."

"What can we do for them?" I asked. "You know the Army unit has done everything they can to protect the cemetery." I knew that the battery had been very respectful of the graves and took great care not to disrupt them.

"They want to go into the cemetery to make sure the graves have not been disturbed."

This would not sit well with the battery commander, I knew. He would have real concerns that the group might contain Vietcong sympathizers who'd be very eager to see how his battery was set up.

"What do you think?" I asked the Vietnamese company commander.

"If it were up to me," he said, "I'd let in a few village leaders to give them assurances. But I can't obviously tell the Americans what to do."

"Okay," I said. "We'll see what the battery commander says."

We went over to the artillery position and explained the situation to the battery commander and his first sergeant.

"Sir," the first sergeant said, "you can't let them in here. If they come in, they're going to see our battery position, our security, and how we're laid out. It's a big risk. We shouldn't do that."

"If we don't let them in," the battery commander said, "how will the people in the village take it?"

"They're probably going to be really pissed off," I told him. "You're going to alienate them, sir." This was an unfriendly area, seriously infested with Vietcong. We were in a real struggle to win hearts and minds. A claim that we had desecrated a local cemetery could be used as a big propaganda wedge.

"What does that mean?" he asked. "Could that help the Vietcong?"

"It could," the Vietnamese commander said. "I can't tell you how important the cemetery of their ancestors is to them. It's the most important element in their religion. . . . But," he added, "I don't want to tell you how to decide this thing."

The battery commander turned to me. "Okay," he asked, "what do you think I ought to do?"

"I can't tell you what to do," I told him. "I have no guarantees that the village elders are telling the truth. I do trust the Vietnamese commander, though, who seems assured that they are. But he can't and won't give you any guarantees either. For what it's worth, I am alone with the Vietnamese all day every day. I trust my life to them."

"God, what a tough decision," he said.

"I know it's not easy, sir," I said, "but we'll support your call. If you don't let them in, I'll try to convince them you're taking care of the graves."

He thought it all over out loud. "I think we should let them in," he said. "We have to show them we are taking care of their ancestors and that we care. It's the right thing to do. . . . But if I take any rounds in the night, even if it wasn't related to their visit, my troops are going to think it was my fault for letting them in. . . . I'll never know for sure."

"You've got to make this call," I told him. "I can't do it for you." The Vietnamese company commander and the first sergeant both echoed me.

After agonizing moments making up his mind, he decided to let the village elders come up into the position—not many, he decided, just a handful.

When they did, they saw that their graves were respected and well taken care of; they were extremely thankful and very relieved. And that seemed to comfort the people in the village.

After they left, the battery commander said to me, "God, I hope we don't get hit tonight, or this week, or anything like that."

"Yeah, me too," I told him. "I'm sharing the hill with you."

Fortunately, nothing happened. It all went okay.

Afterward, I continued to really feel for him. It was an agonizing decision; and I knew that it could some day be my decision to make. (That kind of responsibility came in my next tour, when I commanded a Marine rifle company.) He had to make that call on his own. No one else was going to give him the answer. There was no way he could analyze the situation objectively, no way to get mathematical certainty. And if he made the wrong choice, he'd be sure to face a lot of criticism. He weighed the long-term gain in trust between the Americans and the local people against a short-term risk if the Vietcong gained information that could impact his own troops and came to a decision.

Other military leaders might easily go the other way. If you presented that story as a case study to any gathering of Army or Marine captains, I'd guess they'd probably split 50–50 on the choice.

I don't know how I would have chosen if I had been in his shoes. My inclination would have been to act as he did, but there would have been no guarantees for me any more than for him. A leader has to measure and assess risk, and choose.

Today's leaders have to make many more of these kinds of assessments. Every day, in Iraq and Afghanistan, our military leaders take similar risks to convince the people that they care about their welfare. During a recent trip to Iraq, I witnessed decisions to take down cement barriers, bring aid to the people, take care not to use excessive force, and other measures that could create greater risk to the troops but could win the trust and support of the people. These acts say a lot about the kind of moral leadership our young military leaders display and the risks involved. The day-to-day moral decisions they face in these fights for hearts and minds are a lot tougher than they were in the conventional conflicts of the past.

Military leaders have to look at how the behavior and actions of their troops affect both the enemy forces who may be arrayed against them and the ordinary civilians of the country where their forces are operating. Humane considerations become smart decisions when weighed against what it takes to win today's strange conflicts. Yet actions that commanders feel may be necessary to get at the bad guys may in fact do them more harm than good with ordinary civilians.

Take torture and abuse. There are many good reasons not to torture. Torture leaves scars on both those who perform it and those who are subject to it. If one side engages in torture, the other side is licensed to do the same. Torture and abuse degrade our image and all that we claim to stand for. And their actual ability to gain valid information is at best arguable.

Yet it is argued that if I don't torture this guy, I might end up putting a thousand troops at risk. The argument may prove correct in the short term. You torture the guy, and you may gain a short-term advantage. In the long term, however, torture may cause you to lose moral authority and may make it very difficult to create and maintain a positive image with ordinary civilians. Thus it may result in exponentially greater damage to what you're trying to accomplish.

Though this point is not very often understood, General Colin Powell was thinking along these lines, I'm convinced, when he formulated his now-familiar Powell Doctrine, which asserts that when the nation engages in war, every resource and tool must be used to achieve overwhelming force. This doctrine is frequently misinterpreted. It's correctly claimed that Powell advocates "overwhelming *military* force." But I believe he meant more than that. To Powell, overwhelming force includes a mix of military force, moral authority, popular support, and international legitimacy. He advocates bringing to bear a wide spectrum of overwhelming power, not just military or kinetic power. And he understands that sometimes you may trade off military power to gain moral or international legitimacy that, in a holistic sense, will give you greater overwhelming power.

Leaders who aim to achieve this kind of overwhelming holistic power will face complex and difficult *ethical* choices in those trade-offs.

It's not just the military that faces these dilemmas. Our business laws, such as the Foreign Corrupt Practices Act, forbid us to engage in certain practices that may be legal or accepted in the countries where we are doing business. For example, we cannot pay people who are in positions of influence or pay fees to gain advantages. Where we see inappropriate influence or bribes, others see legitimate "expediting" practices or service fees.

Though our laws may handicap our ability to do business in certain places and give advantages to competitors from nations that don't have such strict rules and laws, I am convinced that they enhance our image—and our business—in the long run. Foreign governments and companies have frequently chosen ethical companies I have been associated with over other companies that follow less strict moral and legal codes. Integrity *does* matter.

EVERY ONE OF US is inundated daily with ethical questions and controversies that catch us up in confusing debate over right and wrong. These questions range all across the public and private spectrums: When is a preemptive war justified? Can our government ever justify suspending civil liberties? How do we define torture? Is it ever justifiable? Who should control the internet? Is it ever right to negotiate with extremists? When does life begin? Does a woman have the right to choose to end her pregnancy? How should we define marriage? Do we have the right to create designer kids? Should we deal with governments that are not democratic? Is there such a thing as excessive profits or executive compensation? And on and on.

Though we may face more of these agonizingly difficult questions today than we did in the past, such dilemmas are not new. Most presidents, for example, faced with major wars suspended civil liberties in some form or other. After the fact, debates raged: Was the suspension right or wrong? Are civil liberties an absolute that must never be touched? Or can conditions arise that require loosening them for the greater good? . . . And then when war came again, civil liberties were likely suspended again—from John Adams's Alien and Sedition Acts, to Abraham Lincoln's suspension of habeas corpus, to Franklin Roosevelt's internment of Japanese Americans, to George W. Bush's Guantanamo Bay, extraordinary renditions, and wiretaps.

Should we have negotiated with the Palestine Liberation Organization, Irish Republican Army, or Libya? How about the Taliban or Iran? Where is the line? How do we square the interests of peace with the justice of accountability?

WHO'S GOOD? WHO'S BAD?

Everyone recognizes that some people are "good" and others are "bad"; and we all—even the bad guys—like to count ourselves among the "good." In the Rolling Stones' song "Jig-Saw Puzzle," the killer goes home in the evening to an ordinary "good" life with his wife and kids. We saw the same thing portrayed in the TV series *The Sopranos*. The difference between "good" and "bad" seems simple enough . . . but then waves of tough questions roll in.

How should ethical questions be decided? Whose principles, philosophy, or religious beliefs should govern our decisions? Should exemptions be made on selected principles in some circumstances? Should we suspend rights we hold dear for a perceived greater good during tough times? What should be the measures of good and bad?

Attempts to answer these questions normally come within some religious or philosophical perspective. While both perspectives have great value, I like to approach ethics from a different direction—as a quality and function of leadership.

When I teach ethics as part of leadership, business, or governance courses, I explain to my students that leaders are responsible for establishing and enforcing the ethical code for the organization they lead. The code may emerge in one shape here and maybe a different shape there—though there will be common elements—but no organization can long exist without some driving ethical code. And it's unimaginable that a code will emerge in full flower from below. The leader must define and promulgate it.

My students always have a hard time with this principle. There's always loud debate and doubting questions. They're nervous about the prospects, as future leaders, of imposing their code on others—perhaps because they're anxious that others will impose *their* code on them. These kids are all good, ethical people. And most have a very strong sense of the line between right and wrong—not yet blurred by age and jaded by experience. Yet I get these questions from them every time I discuss ethics and leadership: "Whose code am I enforcing?" "Which ethical principles do I apply?" "By what authority do I set ethical or moral rules?"

My answer stresses the difference between a set of standards an organization must follow and each person's own private moral code. Every leader has to wrestle with the potential conflict between personal codes and the code of the organization.

How does a leader establish collective ethics? Where does he or she draw the line between setting rules for conduct and dictating individual moral behavior?

These are tough questions, and they grow tougher as modern society becomes more free, as cultures clash, as belief systems are challenged, and as science and technology open up new dilemmas.

We know from experience that a code of ethics produces stronger and better individuals, families, communities, organizations, societies, nations, and world. We seek leaders with strong individual codes that guide their personal conduct; and we expect these leaders to provide the institutions they lead with core values and rules of behavior that make each member of the institution a successful person in a successful organization.

An organization's ethical structure and the processes that support it will also allow individuals within the system to be heard. If not, their grievances will often be addressed from the outside—and will usually harm the organization far more than if it had paid attention to voices from within.

But we still worry about that blurry line. How far into individual or private moral behavior can the organization's ethical structure go? And how far should it go?

At DynCorp, we had employees in Afghanistan and Iraq. Dangerous places! What do we do if the qualified spouse of an employee assigned to a combat zone applies for a job there as well? What's the policy going to be? If you reject the spouse, can they claim that you're prejudiced against married people? "If I weren't married, I could take the position, but because I'm married, I'm rejected." Is that fair? Is it legal?

When we did assign married employees together in a combat zone, serious problems sometimes developed. Infidelity, concern about safety, domestic disputes, and other issues caused headaches for the company.

I was there as the CEO and our lawyers wrestled with these dilemmas.

"You've got to be careful," the lawyers advised—unsurprisingly. "You don't want a lawsuit."

"What can I do?" the CEO asked. "What policies can we establish? . . . How much do I cross the line into personal morality? What is the right organizational ethical code in situations like this?" In this case, he elected to restrict new couples from being hired.

When setting a code, issues like employee relationships, appropriate dress, and appropriate behavior all require a degree of personal judgment. Any code that results will not have universal acceptance and will be challenged.

MAKING DECISIONS ABOUT ethical practices and moral codes is ever more difficult. Not only is there a more diverse group of employees and members than ever before, but there is also greater diversity in how they accept moral and ethical guidance. Answers are clearer when a leader is directly involved with ethical questions about business practices, standards and conduct, contracts, and legal requirements. But there are gray areas even here.

You might find yourself in a situation where you're on solid legal ground but have stepped into behavior that is ethically questionable. This can occur in hiring and firing decisions. You can have sound legal and good business grounds for firing someone, but compassionate or fairness considerations may make the decision ethically questionable.

I've had bosses—God bless them—who have not been willing to go into those gray areas. They're willing to lose money or opportunities rather than cross that line. (I couldn't work with someone who crossed that line.) But they could pay a price in lost business. Keeping to the code you've set is not always easy.

Although it may seem counterintuitive, I have observed that enterprises that place principle over the bottom line or temporary expediency are, more often than not, rewarded in the end. They certainly are rewarded in terms of employee respect, loyalty, and productivity.

While in recent years we have seen seemingly growing numbers of abuses and corruption in both government and business, I don't believe ethical standards have declined. Rather, it's easier today to shine lights on acts that were more easily hidden in the past.

Unrestrained greed is ever a large temptation . . . until its dire consequences fall on everybody's heads. Franklin Roosevelt's words at his second inaugural more than seventy years ago still ring true: "We have always known that heedless self-interest was bad morals; we know now that it's bad economics."

APPROACHES TO ETHICS

Over the course of two thousand–plus years, philosophers have established five ethical lenses through which we can look at the ethical choices that challenge us:

1. *The virtue approach* is based on the principle that the best individuals, our leaders, have developed ideal traits or characteristics—virtues—that will and should guide all their decisions and actions. If we choose good people to lead, we can trust their decisions. We expect that these men or women of high character will exercise the judgment necessary to make correct choices. We hope they'll provide us with the wisdom of Solomon.

2. *The utilitarian approach* attempts to measure the greatest good for the greatest number. It focuses on consequences, where the end result may justify imperfect actions taken to achieve it: The "end justifies the means." This principle has a bad rep, which is not necessarily justified. Perfect means—or even good ones—are not always available. Our choices may only range among degrees of bad.

3. *The rights approach* attempts to base good decisions and good actions on basic human moral and civil rights. This is the American Civil Liberties Union (ACLU) approach, which looks to the individual and his rights as the ultimate good.

4. *The rule of law approach* establishes a code, and we live and decide according to it. It is said we are a country run by courts of law, not necessarily courts of justice.

5. *The common good approach* attempts to make decisions and take actions that most benefit the community or society as a whole. It answers the question: What does the most good for the most people?

Though each of these classical approaches can claim a solid ethical foundation, decisions made according to the standards of one will often conflict with the standards of another.

Few of us, in my view, give much thought to which of the five approaches we are using to make any particular decision. Each of us will probably favor one or two approaches over the others if we think about it (and it's good and useful to recognize and understand which ones we do favor; this further defines us). But in fact, most of us will probably have based choices on all of these approaches at one time or another: This approach seems best here. That approach seems best there. . . . Whichever approach we choose, somebody's ox is going to be gored. If, for example, you base a decision on the greater good, someone's individual rights may be violated. Or if you base a decision on protecting individual rights, you may put the larger community in jeopardy.

That's not to say we advocate situational ethics. Rather, we are acknowledging exceptional circumstances where our normal ethical basis for guiding our actions or judgment doesn't seem sufficient.

CORPORATE RESPONSIBILITY

How do we measure a successful business enterprise?

Most will answer: "It makes a profit."

Well, yes, that's true, but profit doesn't cover everything that has to be said about a successful enterprise. It's probably the most necessary condition for success—without profit, the enterprise eventually dies—but beyond that, profit bears much the same relation to success as "getting people to do what I want them to do" has to leadership.

Success also means delivering the right product for the right price and the right quality. And at the same time treating your customers, employees, and those under your control the right way. Profit gained at the cost of delivering shoddy, poor-quality products or by treating customers or employees badly ensures a failed company, even if it produces temporary survival.

These truths have held for thousands of years, ever since people first began trading goods with other people (although societies throughout history have had very different ideas about treating customers or employees well).

In recent times, our society has been demanding increasingly more than these basic truths from our business organizations, enterprises, and institutions. It's no longer enough to meet compliance regulations and the minimum letter of the law. We want more. We want organizations to look at the consequences of processes and

practices as well as the quality of products. We now believe that organizations have obligations to the society and people among whom
they operate. They must bring some kind of "profit"—or benefit—to
the people and to society. We no longer accept electronics manufacturers or paper companies dumping dangerous chemicals into rivers.
We now worry about carbon dioxide emissions that contribute to
global warming. We now try to prevent overfishing. We are shocked
when we see leaders of failed or failing enterprises take home multi-
million-dollar golden parachutes. We are disgusted when mortgage
loans are offered to people who can't pay for them and then the loans
are packaged and repackaged into bizarre and opaque financial instruments with only tenuous links to backing by real property.

We want the leaders of our organizations to show appreciation
for the environment, contribute to the community, manifest transparent business practices, and be out front in many other areas of
popular concern. We want our leaders to act more "responsibly" than
leaders tended to do in the past.

The term for that attitude is corporate social responsibility
(CSR).

CSR has been interpreted in many ways. It can cover everything
from businesses treating employees properly, to producing a quality
product at a fair price, to looking out for the interests of shareholders,
to investing a portion of profits in the community, to making significant charitable contributions and preserving the environment. It's
clear that society's expectations are moving beyond the legal mini-
mums and that compensation, profits, and behavior are under much
greater scrutiny.

Some say that CSR means that you create a charitable foundation;
you give money to worthy causes; you buy a thousand square miles of
Amazon land in order to save rain forest. These are all worthy actions.

Yet others say, "Wait a minute. Reality has to come before that.
Corporate social responsibility means that you first produce a quality
product that lives up to the customer's expectations, at a reasonable
price; that you treat your employees well; that you provide benefit to
your shareholders; and that you respect your customers." In other

words, your first corporate responsibility is to your business and its stakeholders. It's fine to give $500,000 to search for a cure for cancer, but if you're doing that to improve your image and are not producing the best product for the price, caring for your employees, or paying attention to your customers, your gift is phony.

An ethical code of behavior begins with a deep understanding of the function of your organization. You have to know what it's supposed to do. From that base you must create respect for the organization by building a reputation for quality, consistency, fairness, and honesty. These have to be the underpinnings. And by the way, they're good business.

The good works of the Bill & Melinda Gates Foundation are going to be less meaningful if Bill Gates, the Microsoft guy, is treating his employees and customers badly and producing a product that's overpriced and underperforms. Then the roots of what the organization is about are brought into question.

Wal-Mart takes a lot of heat for its treatment of employees. The company may be providing us with products at the best price on the street, but if it is underpaying employees, refusing them healthcare, and punishing workers who speak up for their rights, then the roots of the organization are rotten. (To be fair, Wal-Mart has recently taken steps aimed at addressing some of these alleged behaviors.)

The offering and delivery of products to consumers has to be a total piece.

Institutions have responded. I sit on a number of corporate and not-for-profit boards and on some of their ethics or governance committees. I've seen ever-increasing emphasis on establishing an institutional ethics code, training members to the standards, practicing the institution's core values, and assessing and enforcing adherence. These practices have become good business. In our much more aware society, decisions on investment and on purchases are now made with similar practices in mind. Consumers may at one time have rushed toward the lure of the lowest price, but today that is no longer their only consideration. The rash of safety issues with Chinese products has cured much of our buy-the-cheapest mentality. Now we are looking at how products are produced—by child labor? in ways that harm the environment? with unsafe materials?—as well as at price.

We have learned that an ethical organization whose leaders establish a strong ethics code—and then live it and practice it—ends up with a more productive workforce that is proud, committed, and morally healthy.

Industries now use internal or external organizations to assess ethical compliance. Consultants come in to run ethical training programs. The question they're looking to answer is not "Do you have rules?" but "Do you live them?" Every organization advertises ethical behavior out of necessity; it's either good for its image or it's required by regulation. Every mail delivery seems to bring in another truth-in-lending or privacy protection statement. Is this *only* creating an image, or is it creating a culture? That's the key question.

Whenever I accept a seat on a board of directors or advisers, I have to take the organization's ethical training course and test—usually online. No one is exempt, from the guy in the mailroom to the chairman of the board.

Employees get similar training, also mostly online, but there are lectures as well, and every employee normally receives an ethics manual that he must become familiar with. The courses are not easy. Their content is usually scenarios and case studies; the tests offer ethical dilemmas: "Now what should you do?" a, b, c, d.

We can measure the effectiveness of these training programs in several ways. We can, for example, look at employee feedback. Employees in most organizations are encouraged to report violations of the ethical code through an anonymous hotline system. The board of directors gets the hotline results by categories: equal opportunity employment, discrimination, corrupt practices, and so on. Almost every board has an ethics committee that oversees the company's ethics program. I've been on a number of these committees; the programs I've seen have impressed me.

Organizations also use what's called in the military "command climate surveys." These examine whether the environment of the company is healthy and if the company is meeting standards and be-having in an ethical way. They ask members about the climate of eth-ical behavior and whether it is lived and applied in everything that is done. Similar surveys are given to customers, partners, suppliers, and others who interact with the organization to see if the external view and the inside view are the same.

All of us are increasingly demanding open, transparent, and trust-worthy institutions. We have grown disgusted and angry that sleazy leaders with no moral character continue to pop up in every part of our society. We want honesty, integrity, and quality. Whether it's in our government, our places of business, our schools, or our places of worship, there is a growing insistence on an ethical code.

SIX

THE LED

Some years ago, I was letting off steam to a wise old career diplomat. He and I had been trying with little success to move into action a cadre of midlevel leaders who were brilliant at impressing their bosses but uninterested in impressing their subordinates. As I expressed my frustrations, he smiled. "The chain of command in any organization," he said, "is like a tree full of monkeys. If you look down from the top, you see smiling faces. If you look up from the bottom, you get a much different perspective."

We have all encountered "suck-ups" like these midlevel leaders . . . and bosses who allow themselves to be moved by the flattery and well-honed persuasive skills that selectively shield them from the valuable input from below. Though the leader may be blind to the suck-ups' actual performance, their peers and subordinates are all too aware of their inadequacies and overambition.

Other failed leaders allow themselves to hear only what they want to hear. Or else their top subordinates only tell them what they want to tell them, and in that way they control decisions.

These illnesses have cures: Instead of discreet—or fearful—silence, subordinates are now openly evaluating leaders. In today's successful, cutting-edge organizations, the led are increasingly encouraged to speak up and pass judgment on their leaders . . . and leaders are listening and shaping up for the better. In cutting-edge organizations, leadership chains have also been increasingly flattened. Eliminating hierarchical layers makes the whole system more responsive and inclusive. The payoff has been better organizations with better leaders who are answerable to all within the organization.

Senior leaders in any organization should be wise enough to understand and appreciate the importance of both views of leadership, the one from the top of the tree as well as the one from the bottom. The top and the bottom of the tree place demands and obligations on senior leaders to understand both perspectives; ignoring either view risks failure of both the enterprise and its leadership. In other words, effective leadership has to be judged from the top down *and* the bottom up. And in today's changing world, there's no way you can ignore the view from the bottom . . . even if you try to. The new led won't let you. How many workplace leadership problems, such as sexual harassment or prejudicial treatment, would occur if leaders knew that they were evaluated from the bottom as well as from the top?

THE GENERATION CHASM

Leaders today are leading a breed of subordinates never seen before. We've attached various labels to them, such as Gen Y or the Millennial Generation—descriptive terms for the newest generation that may seem glib and shallow but that signify changing attitudes and perspectives and shouldn't be underestimated.

In my lifetime, I've observed several generational changes, with corresponding changes in labels: the Greatest Generation, the Silent Generation (mine), Baby Boomers, Generation Jones, and Generation X. Some generations are characterized by the priority they place on material interests, some on their altruistic motivations, and some on their need for self-fulfillment. They are formed and shaped in their adolescent years by the times, events, media, and other changing influences their predecessors did not experience.

Each generation that bounces on the scene challenges the leadership of previous generations, who find themselves trying to lead what they can only see as an alien group. Values and attitudes differ, along with the symbols such as music, dress, and entertainment. These differences exacerbate the chasm between generations and heighten the demand for leaders to better relate to the led.

I never thought much about these labels until I realized not long ago that the next generation, still in school, has been called the "New Silent Generation." I'm not sure why my generation and theirs share the label. Have we come full circle back to my generation? I wondered. Today's generation certainly doesn't seem silent.

That question caused me to focus on the generations in between and how different they are. How much have we adjusted our leadership approaches to better connect to each of these generations and to get the maximum from them? How have we reconfigured the organization, processes, and methods along the way to allow everyone to develop fully based on their differences from previous generations? It seems to me, as I look back on it, that leaders have dictated the answers to these questions and based those answers on *their* own generational preferences. Rather than approaching the standards and goals by relating to the needs and nature of the emerging generations, leaders have wanted to maintain proven standards that they sincerely believed in; they wanted to bend new generations to be just like them.

If these labels actually identify significant differences among diverse groups, I wondered, what does that mean for me and others in leadership positions? How must we interact with this new, faster changing generational diversity in our enterprises?

BACK IN THE MID-1990S, the Commandant of the Marine Corps, General Chuck Krulak, altered the way we broke in new recruits to take into account generational changes that he perceived. Messing with Marine boot camp is risky. The tried and true, even legendary, boot camp process is the stuff of sacred tradition. But General Krulak saw a quality in the new recruits he had never seen before—a quality that called out for a change in our approach to training them.

When I was growing up, I was used to receiving real recognition for my achievements and none for my failures. If my team won the championship, we got the trophy. The trophy went only to the winner. If I won a race, I got a medal. If I came in fifth, I did not. If I failed classes, I didn't graduate. The recruits Chuck Krulak was seeing didn't have these experiences. They'd grown up during a time when everybody got a trophy and everybody got moved along to graduate. Krulak recognized that these new, young Marines needed a challenge that would severely test them and that—if they passed the test—could be recognized as a genuine achievement. He wanted, in his words, "a defining moment" at the end of boot camp where the recruits took on some physically and mentally difficult task whose successful completion would earn them their Eagle, Globe, and Anchor, our Corps' insignia. And he wanted them to do it as a team, all pass or all fail.

From this idea was born "The Crucible," a test of endurance, with little sleep and demanding teamwork. It is an exhausting forced march with full gear and high pressure. At the end of this grueling event, as the sun is rising and our flag is raised, the new Marines receive their insignia—the EGA, as it's known—and are addressed as "Marines" for the first time. They have earned the right to that title. Their response is electrifying. This is a magnificent, moving moment. Young, tired recruits full of pride tearfully accept their EGA from a tough drill instructor who pays them the ultimate respect of identifying each of them as a fellow Marine.

General Krulak's addition to our traditional way of training recruits recognized a new generation. It imaginatively adjusted to their needs and motivation in order to make better Marines, while maintaining the uncompromising standards all generations of Marines have needed to live up to.

Contrast that to experiments during the Vietnam era, when some of the military services relaxed standards in an attempt to buy off the new generation. They relaxed grooming standards, eased discipline, and promoted early. These misdirected attempts to relate had devastating effects on our military.

We all quickly learned what Corps leaders knew: "Don't change the standards and objectives. Change the approaches to getting there."

During the post-Vietnam era, our military was in disarray (for well-known reasons), but we came through because tough, battle-hardened veterans of the Greatest Generation—the generation that lived through and fought World War II—not only knew how to stay the course on maintaining standards but how to connect to new generations with new attitudes.

In the Marine Corps, we had commandants like Louis Wilson and Robert Barrow, recipients of the highest wartime awards for valor, who kept us connected to changing generations of new Marines.

Believe me, the generation emerging from the changes ignited by the end of the Cold War and still rocking us is very different from the generations that preceded it.

I've seen that new breed firsthand in my teaching experiences and in my current leadership positions. We've all seen them: Everybody under thirty seems to have their own web pages; they IM their friends; they watch YouTube (the military services now recruit there!); they download and customize their music; they blog and have an online diary; they visit MySpace; they communicate on Facebook; and they take and send photos by cell phone. For my generation and those that came just after mine, much of this is Greek. If the music is too loud, you may be too old!

These facts have forced older generations to adapt or be left in the dust. They have to understand fast-breaking technologies and how they influence behavior. For leaders, the questions are often: I know where I want to take them, but how do I get them there? or, How do I relate to them, challenge them, and keep them on the same track I'm on?

Not so long ago, without thinking much about it, I dropped a reference to the Cold War in one of my college classes. As I tried to explain how the post–Cold War era was confusing, complex, and dynamic compared to the order that went before it, I got curious, baffled looks. Suddenly I realized my students had never known the Cold War, it had never been part of their experience. It was history, not a reality they'd lived. It seemed like yesterday to me.

Because their experiences growing up had come in the complicated era that followed the Cold War, they couldn't relate to the comparative points I was trying to make. Where had the time gone!

The Cold War had defined most of my life. To me it *was* yesterday!

It soon hit me that these young people had roughly the same relation to my big life experiences as I had to those of my parents. My mother and father lived through the struggle to immigrate from a poor region of Italy to a strange, magnificent new world. Once they'd settled in their new home country, they lived through the First World War, the Depression, and the Second World War. I went through none of that. I grew up riveted by their fascinating stories. Because these stories shaped the way my parents approached the world and raised me, they shaped my life; but I could never personally relate to them. And when I came to shape my own ways of approaching the world, I based them on my own formative experiences, not those of my parents.

This truth holds today as much as it ever has. Attempts to make new generations conform to the older generations' ways of acting and thinking have always been a source of friction.

Now I see successful leaders and enterprises adjusting to the new generation rather than trying to force them to adapt to the old ways. They are capitalizing on the uniqueness of the new led and leading them to the goals desired in ways they can relate to. And it's working.

TODAY'S LED

The led today are more knowledgeable and more assertive than the led have been in the past; and they have more to say to leaders, more influence, more demands, more expectations . . . and more needs. More than ever before, the led have, and want, a say in judging the quality of leadership. Hotlines, command climate surveys, ombudsmen, and many other reporting mechanisms allow them to weigh in on leaders' performance with the view from the bottom of the tree.

In the past, the led avoided leadership and tried to stay anonymous. The old military advice to never volunteer and never draw attention to yourself has long disappeared from barracks counsel and from the workplace. Today's led seek out leadership; they have something to say to it and expectations they want fulfilled.

In simpler days, authority based on position was all it took to get work done. Obedience, subservience, loyalty, and self-discipline were demanded and expected of the led. Scarcely any aspect of their lives did not depend on the leader. If you didn't like the leadership, your only option was revolt. Later, the relationship between managing leaders and the laboring led became more structured. The laboring led were seen as functions, component parts in large, impersonal industrial processes.

Fredrick Taylor, the father of "scientific management" at the turn of the twentieth century, advocated a concept of management control and assembly-line leadership that dominated the way we thought about leading and production for much of the past century. The job of the leader was to watch over and manage the vast machine and to improve its functioning and efficiency. Yet the led were not powerless. The rise of democratic systems protected their rights to organize, unionize, and create counter-rules. Where before there was dependence of led on leaders, now there were contracts. From contracts flowed stability and security and sufficient income to live on. We agreed to have two classes that often interacted on a strained, adversarial basis: white collar and blue collar, officer and enlisted, management and labor.

Today the relationship between leaders and led in successful organizations is, more often than not, close and fully participatory . . . almost unheard of in the past. Leaders listen to the led. They attempt to get buy-in, commitment, partnerships, and a sense of co-ownership (sometimes literally) with the led. Leaders have to know what makes the led tick, what they want, why they do what they do, what defines them, what their aspirations are. Only with answers to these questions can leaders create the productive and motivated teams that are the keys to success in today's world. We no longer build a leadership hierarchy in cutting edge modern organizations. Instead, we build leadership *networks* that make the business of leading institutionalized and multidirectional. Leadership is no longer only vertical, working from the top down. It is distributed, pervasive, invited from all members, and instilled in the culture of successful enterprises. We now seek to build leadership organizations as opposed to organizations with leaders.

The new leadership now emerging increasingly does not appear as an individual and personal quality but as an institutional quality. We now talk of a leadership culture or organization, meaning that the process of leading comes from multiple directions rather than just from the top down. You form a team with multiple skills that needs to be integrated. Each member "leads" from his area of expertise, with a common leadership focus and approach, and contributes to the decision making. There may be one ultimate decision maker, one person who is ultimately responsible and accountable, but more sharing of the input and more delegating of supporting decision making goes on. Organizations now invest a lot in training and educating all members in leadership skills in order to build this common culture.

I have participated in leadership retreats, or off-sites, that are part of structured leader development programs run by innovative companies seeking to develop that kind of leadership culture, to teach leadership skills and provide a challenging leadership environment for all employees. For new generations, this investment in their leadership development has great appeal. They are invited into the organization's leadership process and thinking. They have a say. Their views, judgment, and skills are appreciated and valued. Everyone buys in to leading the enterprise to success.

And the new led are eager and ready to join in this shared leadership concept.

WHO ARE THEY?

When I joined the Marine Corps in 1961, the Marines had a recruiting slogan, "We build men, body, mind, and spirit." It has become clear to me over my several careers that this slogan had an important message beyond the obvious. It recognizes that all of us have three parts in our makeup—three "cylinders" in our being. To run at maximum efficiency, all three must be firing; and all must be developed, satisfied, nurtured, and understood by leaders if they want to draw the most out of their people.

It is my experience that leadership must address these three parts. Narrowly defined leader roles that don't encompass a holistic view of those they lead, and fail to tend to the needs of those parts, will lose the new generations.

Today's led are no longer interchangeable component parts in vast corporate machines. They come in varieties that are culturally, ethnically, linguistically, religiously, racially, and geographically differ-ent to degrees unknown to the generals and great corporate lions of the past. Just look at the last presidential election as a sign of the times. The candidates included an African American, a Hispanic American, an Italian American, a Mormon, a senior citizen, and a woman. That kind of field could not have been imagined a few decades ago.

This diversity is *not* a disadvantage. There is a richness to this di-versity that makes organizations and societies that embrace it far bet-ter. Diversity adds to the organization and its ability to relate to the stakeholders, provides broader insights, and taps into the full poten-tial of its members' potential contributions. The development of our great nation is testimony to that.

But a leader must understand, at the same time, that he will find in such diversity a complex mix of distinct attitudes, prejudices, val-ues, opinions, and heroes and models that will be difficult to manage and to relate to. He cannot make the same assumptions and general-izations his predecessors could. Building cohesive teams today is a much more challenging task.

The new led are not just more diverse than previous generations, they have more knowledge, education, and a better sense of who they are and what they can do. They are increasingly mobile. Unlike their parents, they are much more inclined to pull up stakes and head out for what they perceive as greater opportunities for personal growth and fulfillment. They increasingly see themselves as citizens of the world and are not bound by a narrow, local identity.

In other times, the led exchanged loyalty for security and stability. Today they rarely feel the need for either security or stability . . . or for long-term loyalty. They have shucked the legacy of their Depression-era forefathers. They are risk takers and travelers. They won't ever wonder in their golden years what might have been; they will go after it now!

It may be that today's economic slide will change this pattern. But I doubt it.

In 2008, in my class of forty-three students at Duke University, only two came from North Carolina, Duke's home state. When I looked out at my class, I saw people with South Asian, East Asian, and African (not African American) names. There was a Haitian, an Eastern European, a young woman born in Russia and now an American citizen. There were Californians, Texans, New Yorkers.

When I asked them why they came to Duke, I got answers like these: "I wanted to try something new." "I wanted to get away. I didn't want to go to school locally." They wanted to be free from parental control, like most young people. But they also wanted to be free from the place where they grew up. They wanted to go to a new and different part of the country, someplace entirely different. They wanted new experiences.

The national and international mix was surprising to me but certainly not unusual today. When I looked down the hallways of the two enterprises where I have most recently worked, I saw an equally remarkable mix of diverse peoples filling the offices and cubicles.

Leaders achieve commitment from the new led only through their own deep commitment to understanding and communicating with them and to fulfilling their growing ambitions of self-worth. Leaders can no longer ignore—or make assumptions about—what makes the led tick.

WHAT DO THEY WANT?

In the early 1990s, while serving as a brigadier general in the U.S. European Command in Stuttgart, Germany, the Daimler-Benz senior management led me on a tour of their corporate headquarters. I was greatly impressed with innovations I hadn't yet seen in corporate organizations. All the interior spaces were designed to create the most favorable work environment; the employee child care center was state of the art; the superbly equipped fitness center with personal trainers was available for employees during working hours; the cafeteria offered inexpensive, healthy menus; and the beautifully landscaped campus encouraged employees to take walks during free moments or at least lift up their eyes for a more tranquil view when they were working. The Daimler senior management did not see these features as corporate benevolence. In their assessment, they improved productivity, attendance, positive feedback, loyalty, and longevity with the company. In the past, employers felt that employees had to earn such things as leisure time; now we are recognizing that leisure is a need for a healthy, productive workforce. For organizations that implement them, the investment payoff in these kinds of programs for organizations has to be enormous.

What I saw in that Stuttgart office complex fit what I believed and experienced in the military. We have learned over time that those serving in the military will perform their demanding tasks much better if we care for the whole person, not just the professional soldier. In the military, we pay more attention now to what's referred to as quality of life issues. Attention to psychological issues created by the stress of battle, to family needs, and to providing individual development through education opportunities are just a few examples of how military leadership has addressed these needs.

INNOVATIONS LIKE THOSE at Daimler-Benz—now commonplace—were cutting edge in the early 1990s. Daimler recognized a new kind of employee—an employee who must be respected and listened to.

"The first act of respect is to listen," a leadership consultant once said to me. Profound words. They made me realize how rarely bosses truly listened to subordinates. To me, every person is a story. Every good leader must be genuinely interested in appreciating the story that every person he leads has to share.

We have all encountered leaders who have been endowed with the seemingly magical ability to connect to other people and to show sincere interest in who they are. One of the most significant mentors in my life was a former Commandant of the Marine Corps, General Al Gray. General Gray had that magic touch. Although those he led had countless reasons to idolize him, there was one single standout reason for all of us who knew him: He sincerely cared about us. He *listened*. He always had time to ask about our well-being and hear our views. To him, we were all family.

The value of the feedback from this kind of interaction doesn't come only from the quality of the ideas exchanged but from the very act of soliciting them.

Though paychecks and job security will never go out of style, today's generation of led want more than these basics. They know they have important knowledge and skills to offer the enterprise, and they expect to be treated with dignity and respect. They want their bosses to recognize their contributions. They want to be involved, to be heard, and to have serious engagement with leaders. They want to be challenged, stimulated, and allowed to grow in every dimension.

A friend of mine who runs recruiting for a major corporation was tasked with developing its incentives and awards program. In order to determine how employees viewed the corporation and what they were looking for in the way of rewards, compensation, and recognition, he conducted an employee survey. Its results were surprising. They pointed up a wide difference between Baby Boomers and workers from younger generations. Older employees tended to seek rewards in the form of increases in pay, while younger employees wanted rewards in the form of greater public recognition of their accomplishments—nonmonetary awards such as certificates, plaques, and trophies; they preferred these to larger paychecks. To hear "I'm proud of you" with a handshake from the boss and a photo with him or her is more powerful for them than an impersonal material benefit, especially if the recognition is public, documented, and well deserved.

This new form of recognition came very close to me when my own daughter, Maria, made it clear that I had to be present when she received an achievement award at Vanguard (the mutual fund company) from the then CEO, John Bogle, the legendary founder of the Vanguard Group. The event took place in Bogle's office. During a long chat afterward when he personally expressed his appreciation for her work, her pride and satisfaction were clearly evident. A pay raise alone or some impersonal ceremony would not have had the same effect. As a proud father, I could see how much the personal touch meant to her.

Leaders must realize that watching over the narrow, bottom-line, job-related needs of the led no longer works. They need to address issues such as health, fitness, morale, motivation, mental stimulation, individual development, and sense of achievement more than ever before. For today's led, there is more to life than stability and take-home pay. They personally cherish time and opportunities to develop beyond their workplace environment.

COUNSELING AND MENTORING

I once asked a friend of mine, a recently retired executive vice president for operations at the Bank of New York, to tell me the biggest change he had seen in his many decades in the banking industry.

"Counseling and mentoring," he quickly answered. "Counseling and mentoring are no longer optional. They're expected and demanded by those we lead."

Counseling and mentoring have been with us since humans emerged on the African savannahs. But today they have become more necessary than ever before . . . and more subtle, difficult, and loaded with pitfalls. In the old days, some old guy would take a liking to some younger subordinate, see that he had the right stuff, and take him under his wing. But now mentoring is much more deliberate, much more structured and planned, and a much more significant part of leader development programs. And you see the led seeking it more aggressively. They expect it, and they'll often demand it.

Looking down from the top, we now see organizations thinking harder and acting more deliberately to bring forward and develop their future leaders. They're more and more asking themselves how they can use their own people and resources to teach and train promising subordinates. They're more focused on internal succession planning, and boards of directors designate committees to oversee the process. Even in today's economic turmoil, "Grow your own and keep them" is still the best way to develop consistency, quality, and loyalty in complex organizations.

Organizations are also now hiring professional coaches to develop work as well as life skills in up-and-coming leaders. Even CEOs use coaches.

Counseling, coaching, and mentoring need to be based on a deep understanding of who people are and what formed them as well as on a relationship of mutual trust and respect. These abilities don't come automatically with the rights and privileges of authority and position of leader over the led. Both parties in the process have to be receptive to the substance of the exchange; and both must let down their shields and be open to feedback that can at times be difficult to accept. These actions can expose vulnerabilities that can stress the shared trust and respect.

And counselees have to be open and honest and drop the old advice about turning faults into positives and never admitting a limitation or weakness. Responding to questions about personal weaknesses with the classic answer "Sometimes I work too hard" doesn't work in this environment.

COUNSELING FROM BELOW can be no less important than counseling from above.

Years ago, as a young lieutenant, I faced my first command experience, a Marine rifle platoon. When I introduced myself to my platoon sergeant—an experienced, battle-hardened veteran—he pointed out to me that his responsibilities included making me a better leader. His duty, as he saw it, was not only to implement my orders and attend to our Marines but also to contribute his knowledge and experience to my development as a leader. In other words, his leadership duty was not just focused downward, as a function of a hierarchical structure, but also upward. I hadn't expected that perspective. I then started looking at him, my subordinate, as a valued mentor and counselor. Needless to say, this young lieutenant benefited greatly from that arrangement. I brought education. He brought experience. Sharing our strengths made us both better leaders.

His might have been an exceptional attitude four or five decades ago, but it is expected today. Feedback from subordinates should be as welcome to leaders as counseling from seniors to subordinates. Both aid leader development. Again, it's leadership from all directions in the organization.

My CEO at DynCorp used to end his counseling and performance evaluation sessions with: "Now, how do you evaluate my performance?" This was not BS. He was serious about wanting feedback.

As you can imagine, the first-time counselees who found themselves counseling the boss had interesting reactions. But we all knew him well enough to know he was for real, and we all gave him the honest response he was asking for. I was always impressed by how calmly he accepted and considered even the negatives. He was sincere in wanting to hear how those he led viewed his leadership.

WHY DO THEY FAIL?

When performance suffered in earlier times, leaders searched for ways to force better performance. It was "shape up or ship out." "You need us more than we need you."

Threats like these will probably never go out of style. But today's best organizations and leaders try to determine why their subordinates may not be delivering the performances they expect. The hire-and-fire mentality of the past has been replaced by a developmental approach. We ask questions today that seek to identify causes for deficiencies in skill or aptitude, or for lack of motivation, poor attitudes, inability to meet objectives, or other factors that create obstacles to performance. Solutions come in the form of training, counseling and mentoring, improvement of work environment, removal of obstacles to performance, incentives, and inclusion in decision making.

Successful enterprises now view training and education programs as critical investments in their people; no longer are they considered luxuries that are the first to go onto the chopping block when budgets get tight. These programs have exponential payoffs that many old-school leaders have never been able to realize. In addition to increasing productivity, they build loyalty and improve retention.

FATHER, TEACHER, GUIDE

Leaders rarely fully know the role they play in the lives of those they are privileged to lead.

As a young officer in my mid-twenties, I was hit with this realization one evening on a ship bound for an overseas deployment with my company of Marines. I stepped abovedeck after the evening meal to get some fresh air. As I approached the rail, I recognized one of the best of my young Marines standing there enjoying the breeze. He had just been meritoriously promoted to lance corporal, a true achievement. He was a model Marine and natural leader. I greeted him and told him how proud I was of him. After we'd talked for a while, he paused and looked at me very seriously. "You know, sir," he said, "you're the closest thing to a father I've ever had."

That took me back. Though I was certainly flattered and thanked him for his trust, what really hit me was how we may unknowingly fill important roles in other people's lives. A leader must not assume that his role is limited by what he thinks it is or what it says on paper. It may stretch far beyond the description of responsibilities that goes with the position.

During the mid-1980s, General Gray, our commandant at the time, came out to observe a training exercise involving one of the units of the Okinawa-based Marine regiment that I commanded. As we were standing on the beach watching a night amphibious landing,

he said to me, seemingly out of the blue, "You know, today is a significant date in Marine Corps history."

I had no idea what he was talking about, and wracked my brain
trying to figure it out. A famous battle? A historic innovation developed by the Corps?

I finally gave up and said, "Sir, what is it?"

He smiled. "Today," he said, "for the first time in Marine Corps
history, we have more dependents than we have Marines. Today,
Colonel, you lead more family members than you do Marines."

His words struck me. Of course I was familiar with my responsibilities as a leader to the families of our Marines; yet I had never really
thought much about that. I couldn't help contrasting that reality with
my experiences as a young lieutenant, when only two Marines in my
forty-five-man platoon were married, and one was the platoon sergeant. At that moment in Okinawa, over twenty years later, nearly half
the members of the companies in my regiment were married. And
today the numbers are even higher.

The demands that come with those kinds of demographic
changes drastically alter leadership responsibilities, approaches, and
skills. The complex scope of these responsibilities has brought big
changes not only in the military but in almost every enterprise. Leaders do not have the option to cherry-pick which obligations to accept
and which to ignore. Today, a leader must be a man or woman for all
seasons.

Almost five decades of experience out in the world have taught
me that leadership comes with many more obligations than I imagined when I started as an eighteen-year-old officer candidate. The
leadership experience has become much broader and more complex
than ever before, encompassing aspects of leadership unknown in the
past.

THAT EVENING LONG AGO on the deck of the ship with that young
lance corporal brought to mind words from our *Marine Corps Man-*

ual. They have remained in my mind ever since: "The relationship be-tween leader and led is as teacher to scholar and father to son." The words came from General John Lejeune, the Marine Commandant in the 1920s and one of the Corps' most revered leaders.

I don't believe you can be an effective leader if you don't care about your people. You must value them as family. You must have a genuine interest in their well-being and in who they are and what makes them tick. This is truer than ever before. It is difficult to relate to emerging generations with vastly different outlooks and percep-tions from ours, but it's critical to try to do so if we are to maximize the great potential they possess.

The new generation of successful leaders gets this, and it is paying off for them.

SEVEN

ENVIRONMENT

The Bush administration began its workup to the Iraq War in late 2002 and early 2003—a process I watched in shocked disbelief. "What are they thinking?" I asked myself and those of my friends who had intimate knowledge of the intelligence, the situation, the culture, and the regional dynamics. I had spent most of the previous decade analyzing the threat to the United States from Iraq and its neighbors and planning for a potential Iraqi intervention, including the crucial days and weeks that would follow the toppling of the Saddam Hussein regime; and this crowd was throwing away all we had learned and assuming away every pitfall that would later entrap them. They were describing a fantasy world with their talk of liberation, "flowers in the street," and a "cakewalk" military operation. They failed to understand what those of us who were familiar with the region knew well, that Iraq was a "fragmented society" (a description used by intelligence analysts who worked the assessments when I commanded CENTCOM) that would come apart like a cheap suitcase when it was stressed. They'd trapped themselves inside forces that were much more complex than they'd prepared for.

The disasters did not stop there: The inexplicably poor decision making that followed the initial intervention greatly worsened the bungled analysis and lack of planning that went before it.

Why?

"You break it; you own it," General Colin Powell famously remarked. But where Iraq was concerned, it was more than break it: "You touch it; you own it." As soon as we entered Iraq, we owned all its problems. Not just the security problems. We owned the governance problems, the violence problems, the societal problems, the tribal problems, the infrastructure problems, the humanitarian problems. We owned them all. In for an inch, in for a yard. And our naive civilian and military leaders didn't see that.

"This is a liberation," they insisted. "We're bringing democracy to a region that has only known tyranny. We're not here to occupy. We're here to set them free."

All excellent sentiments. But we brought no liberation. Once we crossed the line of departure, we stumbled, unprepared, into an occupation . . . with *all* the complexities of occupation in such a complex and fragile society.

Certainly our military and political leaders were well intentioned, experienced, and wanted to succeed. So what happened?

They terribly misread the environment. They applied a framework that did not fit reality.

They are not alone in failing to understand the environment in which they are operating, or intend to operate.

Look at the economic meltdown of 2008, and still melting. What happened there? All the economists, financial experts, government regulators, administration and congressional leaders, and Wall Street commentators were at a loss to explain why it happened, how it happened, and what we should do about it. They all looked like a herd of deer in the headlights. They supposedly live and breathe this stuff day in and day out. It is their life's work. Yet they seemed as confused and helpless as we did. Every day we heard the media ask sharp questions that demanded answers: How do we fix this mess? Who's responsible? What do I do about it? How bad will it be? Where's the bottom to this disaster?

No satisfactory answers came from the so-called experts.

It became clear that the economic and financial worlds in which these so-called leaders and experts lived and functioned had drastically changed, and they had missed the changes. The system was far more globalized and interconnected than they realized. They weren't attentive to the risky and unethical practices that were becoming commonplace. They didn't sense that the very foundation of the system was shaky. Was it blind greed, ignorance, rapid and radical change, or incompetence that caught these leaders flat-footed? Or was it all of these?

As this crisis proves, leaders of every kind—in government, corporations, military commands, or academic institutions—function in a much more complex and complicated world today than most of them grew up in. Understanding the new world is critical to survival and success.

"The guerrilla is like a fish swimming in the sea" wrote Mao Zedong, the master of modern insurgency doctrine. "The fish cannot survive without a sea to support it." For guerrillas, he said, the sea is the people. Guerrillas must be sensitive to the people, understand them, and build and nurture relations with them. Unless a significant part of the population backs a guerrilla force, the guerrilla force cannot survive. If a guerrilla falls out of tune with the people, he loses, as Al Qaeda in Iraq discovered when they were rejected by the Sunni population and tribal leadership that had previously tolerated—and often supported—them.

My experience in Vietnam taught me that our adversary, the Vietcong, sought from the people at least one of three reactions: support, fear, or apathy. These conditions created their favorable "sea."

We knew that if we were to prevail, we needed to achieve much more difficult conditions. We needed the people to reject the Vietcong, find the courage to fight them, and/or make a commitment to the South Vietnamese government. It came down to a contest as to who better understood the environment—the people—and how to shape or influence it.

People are fickle and often unpredictable. Toward the end of his life, Che Guevara, the master communist insurgent leader in Latin and Central America, grossly underestimated the environment in Bolivia. He died, defeated at the hands of the Bolivian Rangers, lamenting the failure of the people. They were, as he saw it, "not hungry enough."

The pulse of the people has to be monitored constantly by both insurgents and counterinsurgents. For both, winning "hearts and

minds" relies on understanding and adapting to a very complex environment.

This is true in virtually every endeavor.

How many businesses fail because they don't understand location, customer desires, the competition, or other market realities?
How many fail to see the trends that will lead to their demise if they
don't adapt? Malls replaced downtown shops; reliable, gas-efficient
cars replaced massive guzzlers; and online shopping impacted walk-in
department store sales. If you saw these changes coming, you moved,
adjusted your assembly line, and added Web sites. If you didn't, you
failed.

Any leader who intends for his organization to survive and flour-
ish must be intimately familiar not only with the sea he swims in but
with what he must do to swim in that sea. This requires adaptive leadership. Whether his sea is a battlefield or a marketplace, a leader has
to know and understand all the components that comprise his environment and how they interact and impact his enterprise if he is to
successfully function in it and influence it. If he does not, his organization risks becoming irrelevant in this dynamic, competitive,
twenty-first-century, adapt-or-die world.

At the request of two exceptionally capable leaders, Ray Odierno,
the commanding general of the Multinational Force in Iraq, and Ryan
Crocker, then our U.S. ambassador in Baghdad, I was recently asked
to join a team of experts familiar with Iraq to make an overall assessment of conditions there. As I was briefed on the situation, I was
struck by the number of nonmilitary activities the military command
was involved in. Curious, I put together a rough list of our military
involvement in over fifty major nontraditional military functions:
opening recreational swimming pools; assisting in improving the date
harvest; working to improve electricity output; garbage collection;
water and sewerage improvement; and on and on.

"They include everything from agriculture to zoos, A to Z!" I
joked to General Odierno.

"All of them acknowledge our awareness of the environment
we're operating in," he said with a smile. "If we're going to succeed in

this complex environment, we have to positively affect these kinds of things."

Odierno, Crocker, and Odierno's predecessor, General David Petraeus, have all brilliantly recognized these kinds of things. Contrast that understanding with the assumptions of our leaders in 2003, before we invaded Iraq: As Rumsfeld and company saw it, there was zero need for the military to become involved in the reconstruction and other nonmilitary functions in Iraq. "They don't have to worry about these kinds of things," they dreamed.

The new leadership recognizes the true nature of their environment, and they have adapted to it. As a result, Iraq now has a reasonable chance to succeed.

WHAT IS AN ENVIRONMENT?

An *environment* is the entire space within which an enterprise operates. It includes the nature of the enterprise, its external functions, its influence, its stakeholders, its partners, its resources, its challenges and threats, other enterprises influencing or supporting its efforts, natural conditions affecting it, the competitors, regulators or governing agencies that affect its functions and set the rules, and any other factors, entities, or conditions that impact its functioning. It is a vast sea.

Years ago, many enterprises were mom-and-pop companies that operated in localized, simple environments. They could narrowly and locally define their space and function comfortably within it. No longer. The environment, where just about every enterprise operates—its sea—has become the entire world.

Along with rapid radical change, one of the strongest marks of the new world order is the growing interconnection of environments previously limited to smaller realms. These intersecting environments further complicate any understanding of our space.

U.S. Central Command is tasked to provide stability and security in the Middle East. Because of the worldwide dependency on Middle East energy resources and the growing investment in the region, great interest from people wearing every kind of hat or headgear is focused on the command's actual capabilities to accomplish these goals. While I was commander of CENTCOM in the late 1990s, I received numerous requests from American, international, and local businesses to address and explain these issues.

CENTCOM's security and stability mission gave me the additional responsibility to understand the region's economic dynamics. To that end, I toured oil and natural gas fields, processing facilities, transportation hubs, tanker sea lanes, and other components of the region's vast energy systems in order to better understand how my responsibility for security intersected with this elaborate network and its functions. Another task was to ensure access to the region for the vast seaborne trade as well as for military purposes. The Middle East is the hinge plate of three continents with significant choke points that channel trade routes. If I was to understand my military task, I needed to know how this complex distribution and transshipment network was formed and operated.

I also needed to know the culture: How people thought about things, their attitudes to our presence, and their reactions to our actions were all important to our success and relationships. I had to know the "street." Knowing that street meant seeing through the prism of their culture. In today's conflicts, our military leaders have experts who help them understand what has become known as the human terrain. Teams of anthropologists and others knowledgeable of the cultures and social issues have become as important to a commander as those who provide intelligence on enemy order of battle or terrain and weather.

It used to be that the security or military function operated separately from the other dimensions of power: political, economic, and social. The fighting came first. Then the other dimensions followed once the fighting was over.

After fighting World War II, we moved on to reconstruct economic, political, and social institutions in Europe and Japan. Operating sequentially worked well back in the 1940s, but not today. Today, we must engage in reconstructing societies even as we are still engaged in fighting—not after. And even when fighting has officially ceased, we continue to work to ensure stability and security so that complex economic, developmental, and diplomatic efforts can proceed. Today, we need integrated approaches to conflicts and security requirements; and all leaders—military, political, business, diplomatic—are crying for a more balanced application of the elements of power. Every think tank, congressional committee, and government agency now demands "smart power"—the currently fashionable term that combines "hard" (military) power with "soft" (diplomatic, economic, informational, cultural) power and influence.

Over the last two years, I have participated in half a dozen studies, sponsored by think tanks and government agencies, to determine how best to design, organize, train, educate, and implement better, more integrated, more balanced capabilities for the application of power. Such studies recognize today's changing requirements for conflict and societal reconstruction. Secretary of Defense Robert Gates's pleas for greater funding and other resources for the State Department and U.S. Agency for International Development (USAID) are a clear sign of these changes. It is even more clear that the Obama administration will work to influence world conditions through a greater emphasis on development, diplomacy, and other forms of nonmilitary engagement, which will then be supported by our military might.

More complicated environments are not limited to war-fighting and diplomacy.

In 2008, I completed the strategic plan for DynCorp. We wanted to expand our business into new markets and new international regions.

As I was working through this process, I realized that I needed help understanding which markets were viable for us. Were we headed in the right direction? We wanted to expand into certain new markets with new customers and new regions that were unfamiliar to us but showed promise. Were these opportunities real?

To provide answers to these questions, we hired as a consultant a well-respected expert in market analysis. In addition to his analysis of the market areas where we were currently operating, his company provided detailed analysis of adjacent, complementary, and expanded markets. Without this understanding of the broader space that affected our business—or had our analysis been based on a more narrow understanding of our environment—we would have missed excellent growth opportunities. But each potential opportunity presented more complexity and risk to our business.

Before the consultant arrived, we recognized the need to "sense" our environment, but we quickly realized that our own assessment was not going to get the job done. Our business was complex and dynamic; we needed to make sure we weren't missing or misevaluating something important. The objective, outside set of eyes provided us with the background information we needed before we committed major resources to expansion.

UNDERSTANDING THE BATTLEFIELD

Back when I was a Marine Corps tactics and operations instructor, I used to teach a course called "Combat Concepts." In one part of the course, I covered what I felt were the four principles for mastering the military environment—the battlefield: understanding, assessing, and influencing the environment, and execution (fighting the battle on that prepared, or shaped, battlefield). Commanders not only have to effectively read and understand the battlefield; they also have to sense the dynamics of the battlefield and shape it to their favor prior to and during the fight. (I'll discuss execution—fighting the battle—in a later chapter.)

As in battle, a leader of any enterprise can fail, survive, thrive, or master the field. No leader can be effective unless he clearly knows how to sense the environment, analyze it, influence it, and shape it. The ability to sense it is not enough; the leader also needs to affect his environment.

This process starts with accepting the *reality* of the environment—not what we want it to be but what it *is*. We should not deceive ourselves: Understanding our sea takes time and effort; initial impressions are more often wrong than right; and any influence we can exert over it does not come quickly or easily. Too often I have seen planning that does not credibly assess the operational environment. We push an unrealistic plan, hope, or desire in the face of reality. In the military, we have a name for this kind of major command flaw; we call it "falling in love with your plan." Commanders become reluctant to change or adapt in the face of an environment that is causing their plan to fail. They remain in denial and don't want to adjust or adapt to the reality that is rendering their plan ineffective, or worse.

One part of my job when I taught military tactics and operations was to run simulations for the junior officers. In these exercises, they often fell into a classic trap.

Let's say you're a junior officer up against an enemy in a computer simulation exercise. You first design a scheme of maneuver: You consider assigned tasks, opposing forces, terrain, weather, timelines, and all the other elements you need to form a course of action. Then you execute the scheme of maneuver and move into the attack. After a while, you become aware that the attack is going slowly. You're slugging it out. You're accepting casualties. But you're not meeting your timelines. You're not moving forward at the pace you wanted.

Yet you are achieving a degree of success. You're advancing, and you're gaining terrain.

What to do?

You keep staying with it. Even though you're ever further behind your timelines and your forces are suffering slow attrition, you keep staying with it. You keep staying with it. You keep staying with it. Why? Because there's a minimal degree of apparent success. What you don't see is that, over time, the attrition, the slow bleeding of your force, is going to put you at a point where you've lost more than you gain. It's going to be a Pyrrhic victory at best.

Because all this is stretched over time, it's hard to see.

Junior officers get sucked in by the ability to make progress and move along. They are processing terrain and enemy forces and missing the objective. That mind-set is the trap—the inability to step back and say: "This is a loser's strategy."

If junior officers had a clearer operational or strategic view of their environment, and if they had projected more clearly forward in time and space, they would have recognized the long-term implications that doomed their plans.

What to do?

When you see that you're taking a loser's course and that your line of attack is not productive, you have to look for other options. Most often, you probe and move on multiple fronts. You find the line of attack that gives you the greatest opportunity. You find that gap in the lines where the enemy is weak or vulnerable. You reassess the environment.

If your analysis doesn't reveal an opening, you probe to discover one.

As Eisenhower said, "Plans are nothing, planning is everything." That is, you learn about your environment through the process of planning. Though the product—the plan—may not survive the fog and friction of war, if it's done correctly, your planning effort will give you the depth of understanding to adjust, react, capitalize on opportunities, and foresee challenges. Fall in love with the *planning*, not the plan!

My time as an adviser in Vietnam taught me to appreciate the total complexity of the battlefield beyond my perspective as a Marine lieutenant in a fighting unit. I experienced the many different dimensions of the environment that had profound effects on war-fighting. I learned to sense the broader scope of the conflict and the need to do more than just win the firefights. This education stayed with me. In Vietnam, we won every battle but lost the war. That was a bitter and confusing outcome for those of us who fought so hard and gave so much there.

Jump forward to the present. Now we see that CENTCOM's current commander, General Petraeus, has learned the parallel lessons that apply to the complexities of counterinsurgency and conditions in Iraq. In recognizing that the war in Iraq cannot be won militarily, he has demonstrated a deep and broad reading of the environment he faces together with an equally brilliant understanding of the limits of military power in that environment. He saw the interconnections of the kinetic and non-kinetic functions of that battlefield.

Hence he not only built up the military's security presence in Iraq, he increased its nonmilitary functions to include activities like engagement with tribal leaders, support of essential services for the population, and development of local businesses. When I was in Baghdad, I saw that the daily briefings of the military operations center normally included far greater numbers of tracking statistics on those nonmilitary functions than would be expected. Amazing stuff!

Pentagon leaders whose critically flawed initial decisions about the Iraq war and its aftermath foolishly based their decisions on over-rosy, simplistic assumptions. They fell in love with their flawed assumptions, concepts, and plans. What seemed logical from Washington was not logical on the ground in the Middle East.

What may seem logical from corporate headquarters may not be logical out there where business is done.

The leader can never stop asking hard questions about himself, his organization, and the sea he and his organization swim in. And he can never be satisfied with the answers. It's too easy to believe the sea is the one we want, or that the sea will stay constant and calm.

When my son Tony, then a Marine captain, returned from a tour of duty with an infantry battalion in Iraq's Anbar Province, I picked him up at Camp Lejeune, North Carolina, to drive him home for a much-deserved leave. During the drive, we talked about his experiences. "From your point of view as a junior officer out in the field," I asked him, "what's the war all about? What are the centers of gravity, the things that count? How did you sense conditions in Anbar?"

"From what I experienced," he answered without hesitation, "it's all about tribes, power, money, jobs, and guns. Who controls or influences those has the true power and the greatest chance of success on the ground."

With a father's natural pride, I was impressed with my son's simple, clear, and brilliant analysis of what mattered in the environment where he was operating. Was the senior military leadership's understanding of what they were immersed in and what it took to prevail in that complicated mess as clear as my son's and his fellow junior officers'? I wondered.

I can now answer yes to that question. My visit to Baghdad in October 2008 convinced me they finally get it at the top as well.

WHERE DO YOU FIT?

It's important for leaders not only to understand their environment but also how they fit within it. And this understanding also includes an assessment of how the enterprise stacks up against the competition in its given field.

A leader must ask himself questions like these:

- What are the barriers to entry into my field?
- What are my signature capabilities or strengths, how relevant are they, and how do I retain their uniqueness?
- What are my limitations and weaknesses, and how can I mitigate their negative impacts?
- Is my environment changing, and am I adapting to meet the changes?
- Are my people and organization best prepared to deal in the current environment?
- How strong is my competition?

When I was the executive vice president at DynCorp, I quickly learned that our key to success was to hire, train, motivate, and retain the quality people who could perform the missions contracted for on mostly foreign sites.

Several companies competed for these contracts. There was no barrier to entry in that field. There were no patented or complex technologies, no complicated business models, and no other exceptional barriers to overcome. If we were going to be competitive, we had to put on the table a proposal that was solid enough to win the contract, and we had to perform with maximum effect and efficiency in the field. The good, experienced people who were capable of performing these tasks were sought after by us and our competitors. Anyone with sufficient capital could "buy" the best people. Understanding that environment meant focusing on that workforce. That focus was our strength and our path to success. Our center of gravity was the people, the program managers, we put in the field.

This kind of government services business, I soon came to realize, was much like my experience in the infantry, where our "weapon" was the men of the unit. In armor, artillery, or aviation, the weapons were machines that their men operated. Not so in the infantry. In the end, we put men on the objective, not only bombs or rounds. This required a different way of thinking about our environment and what it took to succeed in it.

From the lowest to the highest levels of military leadership, before plans are made and orders issued, we have to go through a process called an "estimate of the situation." Though these estimates become more intricate and elaborate as you go higher up in command—a simple, short mental process for a squad leader or an elaborate multi-page document for a theater commander—the component parts are basic to all levels: We analyze the mission we're given to glean the specific and implied tasks we must accomplish. We judge the enemy's strengths, capabilities, and vulnerabilities. We analyze the terrain and weather. We assess our own capabilities and resources. We examine the time and space constraints we must deal with. And more recently, we have added an assessment of the cultural environment we are operating within.

A process like this, adapted to your particular enterprise, should be routine in every endeavor. Your world may be changing or shifting under your feet. If you don't have the process in place to constantly sense and influence the changes, you'll miss opportunities and become vulnerable to challenges and threats.

How can I influence my field of endeavor? What power do I have?

Leaders must constantly ask themselves these questions, and others related to it: Can innovation, a change in business practices, an

alternate model, a new market, a new product, a reorientation of resources, a restructuring, or any other action make me more successful or protect me in a changing environment?

How did the U.S. automobile industry so badly read the environment and foreign competitors read it so well?

When I recently visited Baghdad, the concentration by our civilian and military leaders on their degree of "leverage" to influence
events made it clear that they now understood what it would take to
succeed. Yet I also saw that they realized that their ability to control,
enable, or influence events had diminished. Not only, as the old military saying goes, does "the enemy get a vote," but an emerging Iraqi
government feeling its oats—or, more accurately, its sovereignty—
was becoming ever less subject to our influence.

For leaders, knowing your power to influence your environment
is crucial. I've seen too many leaders deceive themselves into thinking
they control more—or less—than they actually control.

The automobile industry has little influence on the price of oil,
yet that price is critical to their business. They must adapt to a critical
component where they have little or no leverage.

Another classic error is to believe that knowing a lot means you
control a lot. We collect massive amounts of information. Great! But
what counts is what we do with it. I have sat through hundreds of exhausting op center briefs filled with thousands of PowerPoint slides
attempting to satisfy commanders' insatiable demands for more stats
and data. All too often, commanders come to believe that command
of the data equates with command of the environment. A potentially
deadly mistake.

As a young officer in Vietnam, I marveled at the color-coded
maps and lists of statistical information I observed during my rare
visits to command posts: maps showing green-shaded "pacified"
provinces, and lists showing impressive numbers of weapons captured, enemy killed or captured, and medical and dental programs
conducted in villages. All very awe-inspiring. Victory was in the making. How could you think otherwise? Unless you were out there in the
battlefield. Out there all the impressive stats and color-coded maps

didn't match the reality I was experiencing. The world so neatly portrayed in the command center often does not represent the real world on the battlefield. Or in the market.

The best leaders are out and about. They don't rely on the mesmerizing lure of statistics and data. They value the sights, smells, and touch from the front to sense their "battlefield." They are at the retail outlets, on the factory floor, on the loading dock, visiting cubicles and offices, and talking to the customers. They have developed that sixth sense that Napoleonic generals and German military leaders have often described in their writings. They know the touchstones they need to feed that sense.

From time to time, I get calls or I'm asked to meet with seasoned senators, such as Chuck Hagel and Ted Kennedy, or other congressmen and congresswomen from both political parties, to chat about conditions in regions of the world that I'm familiar with or on issues where I have some knowledge. I'm certainly not the only person experienced legislators go to for opinions. The good ones all run the traplines in order to get a variety of takes on events and issues and a representative mix of up-to-date views. This is a useful approach. It gives them a constant check on environments they're interested in and allows them to test for new conditions. I've always been impressed by those who take the time to put their ear to the ground and make the continuous assessments necessary to stay abreast of dynamic environments. Listen then decide. This sequence is often missing from leadership that makes decisions then seeks justification rather than knowledge.

TOO MANY LEADERS out there today have misread their world . . . *too many failed leaders.* A rising few, however, are succeeding in this confusing sea of change. Why? They make a concerted effort to understand the changing environment. They embrace the new world and adapt, and they don't curse the darkness or the confusion. They are innovative and opportunistic. They are not reactive. They won't let this world pass them by.

EIGHT

THE ENTERPRISE

I've been fascinated with organizations and their design ever since my first class on the Marine Corps Rifle Squad when I was a young officer candidate. The why and the how of that small but unique organizational structure instantly caught my interest.

The Rifle Squad was developed early in World War II out of the combat experience of veterans of World War I and the Caribbean Banana Wars of the 1920s and 1930s, as well as months of study and field experimentation at our Quantico Marine Base. The aim was to create units to form a Marine Raider organization that could launch strikes in the Pacific theater of operations. The logic of the structure, equipment, formations, and tactics all proved their worth on Pacific beaches.

There were to be three four-man fire teams in each squad. This structure allowed the squad leader to either weight his base of fire with two teams and maneuver with one or weight the maneuver element with two teams and his base of fire with one. Each team was built around an automatic rifle, the famous Browning Automatic Rifle (BAR), as its core firepower. Before the development of the Rifle Squad, fire teams had contained three members; a fourth member was added to each team in anticipation of the casualties that would be suffered during the beach assaults on Pacific islands, where replacements could not be brought forward until the beachheads were seized. These were not the only considerations that went into the structure of this relatively small tactical unit. Even the formations the unit could assume in given situations while retaining its organizational coherence were carefully thought out.

Later, in Korea and Vietnam, the structure was modified to accommodate new weapons systems, such as the grenade launcher, and the demand for new tactics.

A squad may seem like a small, relatively inconsequential organization, but I was impressed with the ingenuity, analysis, and logic that went into its design. As I came to know larger and more complex organizations, I grew to realize how many of them had been created with far less thought and insight—a lesson in developing the right kind of organization for accomplishing the mission and adapting it to the unique environment faced.

My fascination with organizations has never diminished.

I've studied the organizational design of every enterprise I have been part of, and I've greatly profited from the courses I took in organizational development and effectiveness on my way to a graduate degree in management and supervision. When opportunities presented themselves, I redesigned organizations, consulted on organizational design, taught classes in organization and structure, and took part in studies on the subject. Whenever organizational issues rose to the surface or became open to reexamination, I dove in. Early on, I recognized that if a leader can't define or describe his organization down to its inner workings, he can't lead or control it.

The Marine Corps Combat Development Command at Quantico, Virginia, develops the Corps' requirements in experimentation, concepts, doctrine, manning, training, education, equipping, and other component parts. This large, complicated organization—which was born out of the vision of one of our most innovative commandants, General Al Gray—has evolved into many forms over the two decades of its existence. The command took on added responsibilities and missions over time, and the organization grew and expanded.

I became its deputy commander in the early 1990s, while it was under the command of Lieutenant General Chuck Krulak. When

Chuck took over, he ordered a full examination of our command. He knew our mission was critical to determining the kind of Marine Corps we would need in the future, and he wanted to ensure we were properly organized for the task. A specialized consulting group embarked on a multiweek project that dug into every aspect of the organization. The results were eye-opening.

Many processes, we learned, functioned far differently than we thought or intended; and there were many more disconnects in the structure and other elements of the organization than we suspected. But there were also areas that worked exceptionally well.

The Corps needed to know that our processes were interconnected in the appropriate way to ensure that these components fell into place in the right manner and right sequence needed to execute the concept. You can't, for example, field a piece of equipment before you have trained troops ready to operate and maintain it. You can't have the troops available before you have the training programs, facilities, and resources in place to prepare them; and you can't do that unless you've budgeted and programmed for it. The sequence and synchronization were critical. Getting all this right was the mission of our command.

Were our processes properly lined up? Were they in the right order and sequence? Were the priorities right? Were the resources correctly allocated and distributed?

Gaining these answers required a detailed analysis of our organization to ensure it was properly structured to arrive at the right answers.

What was most enlightening to me, as the consultants dissected our organization, was the exhaustive mapping of this complex, intricate structure—a detailed display and analysis of how it was all connected. The processes, relationships, functions, lines of authority, and other components were thoroughly diagramed and explained. I clearly remember the huge diagram rolled out over a large conference table. It looked like the blueprint for a large, complex piece of machinery.

Years later, after I retired from the Marine Corps, I participated in a series of studies on organizational design sponsored by an agency in the Department of Defense. We examined the entire organizational spectrum of combat unit command and staff elements—from organizational structure to processes used in systems that supported operational decision making to the psychological processes involved in the decision making. (The renowned decision psychologist and author Dr. Gary Klein was a member of our study group; his studies of decision making under stress were invaluable.)

In another study and experiment I was involved in at the Joint Forces Command, the military command responsible for developing our joint operational concepts and structure, we set up collaborative staffs that met and planned in virtual organizations constructed purely in cyberspace. The purpose was to do simultaneous planning, combining several levels of command, in order to save time and to improve coordination. Although the initial trials were rough (it was hard for those who'd used old processes for years to adjust to change), the new approaches slowly began to improve and speed things up after we had more practice.

As we went through our detailed work, it was clear to me that combat commands were organizing themselves in ways we had never seen before—the same organizational metamorphosis that I have observed in other successful enterprises.

Leaders who are organizing combat commands, like leaders of organizations everywhere, have realized that our fast-changing world requires new approaches and new thinking: We now see virtual organizations formed in cyberspace, collaborative organizations that connect through information technology to conduct their functions, and new and original forms of teaming with multiple lines of authority. The standard, timeworn mechanical models no longer describe organizations; we now think in terms of biological models. Components in modern organizations are not, as in the past, understood as wheels, cogs, or gears but as living entities that grow, evolve, or adapt.

UNDERSTANDING THE ORGANIZATION

What is an organization? It is a complex entity that operates in a definable environment and is designed for a specific and common purpose. Its elements include leaders, led, structure, processes, support systems, culture, missions, rules, standards, stakeholders, and other components.

A wise new leader entering a new organization takes the time to dissect his organization, as we did at Quantico, and to fully understand and master these complex components. This has to be a first order of business. After all, how can you lead what you don't first know and understand?

A leader should not accept the organization he enters on its face and assume it runs as advertised. His first act should be to delve into its bowels and see how it is structured and running. The charts and written operating procedures may bear no relation to the organization's real mode of operations. This is especially true of organizations that have been around for a long time and have not had a recent review of their structure and operations.

The enterprise cannot run the leader. The leader must run the enterprise. To run it, he has to know and understand it to its core. He has to be willing to change it, reorient it, adapt it, and keep it competitive and relevant in order to meet the new demands of a fast-paced competitive world. An organization's structure cannot become so hallowed that it is allowed to become obsolete or irrelevant. Overvaluation of tradition and fear of change often prevent us from adapting organizations to the environment. The organization is, after all, just a means to accomplish the mission, or purpose, of the enterprise. The organization is not the end state. Accomplishing the mission is.

Leaders should ask questions about their organizations, such as:

- How does it work?
- What does each member do, and how does that contribute to the mission?
- What are our core competencies or signature capabilities, and how are they prioritized in the organization?
- What is the organization's center of gravity, its sources of strength?

- What are its weaknesses?
- What is the rationale or logic to its structure and processes, and when was it last reexamined?
- What systems and facilities are truly needed to support the organization, and when did we last review these requirements?

A mark of successful modern enterprises is the innovative ways they have adapted to become more effective, efficient, and competitive. These changes aren't easy. Except for those younger members who can adapt to constant change, most members cling to stability and consistency.

Some years ago, I was an executive at a company looking at a major reorganization. The head of one sector of the company came into my office totally beside himself. He was in flames. "This is wrong," he kept saying to me. "It won't work."

"Why won't it work?" I kept asking him. "What's wrong with it?"

He couldn't give me a reason. He had no discernible reason for damning the new process.

After a time, it hit me that he did not find fault with the rationale for the reorganization; he didn't *want* to change. His comfort level was in a company structure he had known for many years. He was resistant to change because the need and benefit for change did not outweigh his need for operating in ways he knew and understood. We were taking him out of his comfort level.

Older leaders often oppose reorganization because it removes a familiar system they have mastered and puts them on the same plane with younger leaders. It creates uncertainty and undermines their confidence to lead in a new environment. In their eyes, they are losing the advantages of their longevity and experience. This is threatening. It blinds them to the need for, or the benefit from, change.

BECAUSE ORGANIZATIONS CAN stagnate or evolve in illogical ways, they need constant reevaluation. They are built over time into structures that are rarely fully thought out or planned . . . structures that are often only tenuously rational—pieced together into Rube Goldberg-like mazes of complicated systems. This is especially true of large organizations, whose structural logic can be lost over time and as parts are added, modified, or deleted.

The bloated bureaucracy of our government perfectly exemplifies a ponderous, labyrinthine organization. Except for adding appendages that further expand the bureaucracy, our government defies change.

The last significant revamping of the overall structure of the United States Government to meet the demands of changing times was accomplished more than fifty years ago with the National Security Act of 1947. Plenty of change has occurred in the world since 1947, but aside from limited fixes in specific areas (such as the Goldwater-Nichols Act of 1986), our government has not changed with it. It remains very well organized to take on the challenges of 1947, not those of 2009 and after.

The Goldwater-Nichols Act restructured and re-formed the military, integrated the military services' war-fighting capabilities, and sparked a revolutionary reshaping of one element of government, the Department of Defense. This was good for the military and good for the country. But almost a quarter of a century has passed since Goldwater-Nichols. Threats and missions for our military have radically changed. And the U.S. military, arguably the most adaptive element in government, also struggles with adapting and changing to meet and control these new challenges. Our military is overpowering in traditional conflicts—but far from overpowering in today's more shadowy, complex, nontraditional conflicts. Fortunately, it is a learning organization and can adjust—as leaders such as General Petraeus and others have done recently in Iraq.

IN ORDER TO FULLY understand today's organizations, you have to understand their three major facets: the structure (how it is built), the processes (how things work), and the systems support (whose heart is normally an organization's information and communications systems). In today's dynamic, fast-changing world, you can't ignore these key parts. You have to understand them and make sure you keep them in sync, up to speed, and adaptable. If the nature of the business or the environment where it operates changes, the organizational structure has to morph and change; and the organizational processes and systems technology have to change along with it. Mastering and controlling the organization and making it adaptive are the keys to survival and success, and critically required leadership skills. All this has to be done efficiently, ensuring there is no waste, bloat, or excess capacity. As a rule, you can't compete unless you are leaner, smarter, and faster than your competition.

These changes have to be made carefully, and the impact on the total organization has to be fully understood. I remember a wise general I worked for, a highly regarded expert on manpower issues, patiently listening to young officers shooting out a lot of "good ideas" about how they'd fix the manpower system. These ideas all sounded great and logical—until the general systematically shot every one of them down. All of them turned out to be partial fixes for single pieces of the system. None took into account the needs of the whole. "Every organization is a complex set of interconnected gears of all sizes," he told me afterward. "If you turn one slightly, you might find as a result another one along the chain that is rapidly spinning out of control."

That lesson registered with me. You always have to take into account the whole entity before making changes to one part.

UNDERSTANDING THE STRUCTURE

In the past, structuring an organization depended on control, clear lines of authority, consistency, and uniformity. Little change was welcomed or required. The classic block-and-wire diagram of tiered, layered, stove-piped, or functional structural designs accurately modeled most organizations. The executive function, which unites and directs the whole enterprise—gets the single box on top. Lesser and more specific functions (that is, departments, divisions, or agencies) are placed below the top, each in its own functional box linked by a "wire" to the one above. Departments, divisions, or agencies that are functionally equal in the organizational hierarchy occupy the same tier in the chart. The Chief Financial Officer and the Chief Operations Officer might occupy the tier directly below the CEO. Other functions would then report to each of them: for example, Finance and Accounting, Human Resources, Information Technology and Facilities, Contact Administration, and Planning might report to the CFO.

This very logical system worked well for a long time. But because it was a top-down, directive design, it lacked integration, adaptability, and flexibility.

Today, any student in my classes who gives me a block-and-wire solution in organizational exercises fails the exercise. Block and wire is yesterday's news.

Successful organizations are now flattened, streamlined, and integrated. They don't rely on adding structure to add capability. Instead, they leverage technology to improve or develop processes, or they temporarily build teams from within the organization to meet a requirement. They thrive on being dynamic and adaptive rather than struggling to hammer a preexisting structure to fit swiftly changing challenges. They resist the old block-and-wire diagrams. They now use smaller, integrated structures such as matrix, web, or network organizational designs, multiple lines of authority, and many other forms of structuring that would confuse and dismay those used to old methods of organizing.

Not long ago, I was chatting about organizations with successful businessmen and women at a social event. One, who worked for a highly successful software company, described his office as a large, open warehouse. "There are no partitions," he said. "Everyone, including the bosses, is in the open, and all our desks, filing cabinets, and other office furniture are on wheels. With each new contract, we reorganize ourselves. We roll everything here and there, as needed. Or else we might roll everything around when we want to adapt to new and improved organizational ideas."

"That is the ultimate organizational flexibility and adaptability!" I thought.

UNDERSTANDING THE PROCESSES

Within any organization, complex and often overlapping and intersecting sets of processes make the enterprise function. They must run in harmony for the enterprise to work properly.

Processes may include the ways an organization's members are brought into the organization, socialized, and later recognized, counseled, trained, and developed; the conduct of its operations; relationships with stakeholders and outside entities necessary to its function; the way data is processed into usable information; the way teaming is accomplished; the way intra-organizational communication is accomplished; and many other principal or supporting functions necessary to run smoothly and accomplish the mission.

These processes operate under sets of rules, standards, procedures, and regulations that are based on internal or external codes, laws, and values. Their effective functioning, and the principles that guide or direct them, are central to success, morale, and the growth of the organization.

Some organizational processes are easily observed and normally run as leaders expect and direct. Some are not so obvious and run underneath the leader's radar. And some few of these could actually run contrary to policy or direction and may constitute a "shadow" operation—the real way things are done around here.

This truth was brought home to me yet again during a conversation with the general in charge of the Abu Ghraib prison sometime after the atrocities there were made public. She explained to me that she did not have full control of that facility and her people. It was denied to her. Nor did she have the access or control necessary to delve into all the functions at the prison. Other authorities controlled sensitive procedures for which she had no responsibility. Yet she was held accountable for all the problems and failures at the prison. It's hard to say to what extent the division of authority at Abu Ghraib contributed to the dysfunctions there. Obviously investigation findings revealed that actions were being taken that no element of leadership was aware of.

It behooves a leader to dig into the depths of his organization to make sure he knows how things actually work. He cannot master the organization, control it, affect its course, or ensure its effectiveness and efficiency if he doesn't know how the processes and systems work and interact and if he doesn't have the authority to make fixes.

UNDERSTANDING SYSTEMS SUPPORT

Today, information and communication systems are supercritical to every organization . . . and complex almost beyond comprehension. Advances in technology come so fast and furious that today's cutting-edge information technology may be as passé tomorrow as silent movies.

Many organizations fail because they have not kept systems up to date and responsive to real needs.

IT obsolescence takes several forms. Some systems kluged together out of accumulated legacy products become too problematic and expensive to replace, even after they have lost their ability to support the running of the organization. Many systems are not user friendly and waste valuable member time and effort. Older systems are much slower. When coupled with newer, state-of-the-art systems, they become a drag—much like the old naval saying, "The convoy is only as fast as its slowest ship."

I've seen too many organizations whose systems support can no longer meet the demands required for success. This realization usually comes after a failure, or near failure, and is rarely foreseen. Time and resources lost to correct the problem at that late point only add to the problem, and the costs of upgrading become great.

No organization can ignore technology. It is vital for making an organization viable, competitive, and current. But there are also intangible components to a successful organization, such as its morale and culture.

UNDERSTANDING THE CULTURE

One function of leadership is to create and nurture a common organizational identity, sense of common purpose, mutual support, and feeling of acceptance. The leader is the primary factor in shaping the "culture" that bonds everyone who makes up the organization's team.

We've all known of losing teams in every sport that have the playbook down cold, successful training programs, the best equipment, and superior talent at all positions but lack the intangible qualities necessary for victory. They get high ratings before a season but never live up to the hype. We've also seen the surprise, Cinderella teams that play above their expected skill levels. Something seems to drive them to play beyond the unimpressive capabilities identified on paper. A mysterious team bonding, cohesion, sense of pride, and spirit seem to grab the organization. Invariably, there is no mystery about this. The team's leader is the real driving force behind the apparent magic. He may be the coach, the official team captain, or just some guy with a forceful personality who takes charge.

In successful organizations, the leader identifies and personifies the intangible factors, such as morale, spirit, and pride, that drive the organization and give it energy, direction, and adaptation. If members buy in to and take pride in an organization's identity, then they are likely reflecting the leadership.

Even though the leader is the primary source of influence on an organization's culture, he is not its sole source. It is also created by the processes that drive the enterprise's functions. You can't separate the two. Good leadership cannot overcome malfunctioning processes, and excellent functioning will not overcome poor leadership. A car has to have an engine and wheels as well as a driver. Institutionalized excellence and performance are the goal. How do you make best practices, innovative solutions, and superior functioning routine? That is the challenge.

Forming a stable organizational structure, identity, and culture is not easy in today's fast-changing world. In days gone by, you could seek to plateau and level off while maintaining effectiveness and stability. You could catch your breath for a while and enjoy a level of success. That's rare today: The competition will rapidly catch up or present a new challenge, or the environment will quickly change. You have no choice. Even as you move successfully to one level, you need to be planning your next move.

One not-always-happy result of this need for swift action is constant deal making that results in mergers, acquisitions, partnering, and other relationships that continuously challenge organizational identities. Mergers often flop when incompatible corporate cultures fail to marry happily, as when AOL merged with Time-Warner or when Daimler-Benz merged with Chrysler.

Change, restructuring, expansion, and many other characteristic factors of today's dynamic environment in all fields can also be unsettling and work against creating a desired organizational identity and cohesion.

As a board member of a large corporation that is constantly expanding, acquiring, and reorganizing, I have been impressed with the effort and commitment the leadership puts into maintaining and transferring the corporate culture and identity. Attention to the smallest details of branding and welcoming convey a "family" environment.

I said something to the CEO about this.

"It's not just a nice and right thing to do," he answered. "It's critical to retention and productivity in this business. We need highly skilled engineers with security clearances, a sought-after and extremely valuable commodity in this industry. You have to make them feel they are part of a large, happy family."

Large, impersonal bureaucracies have difficulty generating a positive organizational culture. Most government departments and agencies have shaped and developed their organizational identities, cultures, and approaches to dealing with challenges over many decades . . . plenty of time to grow rigid, throw up barriers to other agencies and departments, and become virtually impervious to change. In spite of leaders who do everything in their power to make the relationship work better, the State Department and the Department of Defense rarely work well or easily with one another. The chaos that followed our initial military success in Iraq in 2003 would have been far milder if State and Defense had formed focused, integrated, collegial teams that developed well-thought-out policies and provided for their execution on the ground.

BUREAUCRATIC BLOAT

Can we eliminate bureaucracies? Should we?

As much as we might like to, we can't walk away from highly structured organizations. Certain functions require organization and even bureaucracy—the most structured of organizations. The Internal Revenue Service and the Department of Motor Vehicles have to be bureaucratic. They have to be mechanistic, process oriented, and layered.

Just mention the DMV, and everybody groans. You enter a vast, soulless, Kafkaesque space, you face long lines, and then you deal with people who are rude on their good days. But the DMV usually gets the job done efficiently. It issues licenses to millions of people and ensures people are qualified to operate vehicles. It's hard to streamline that kind of organization. You can make it more efficient, friendly, and acceptable. Certain actions require process (though you can put much of it online); and that requires structure. Strong, heavily processed organizations inevitably end up becoming bureaucracies.

Problems with bureaucracies come when they aren't examined constantly and rethought and updated; and then they become stifling. They become inefficient.

Back in the 1980s, I was a lieutenant colonel, recently selected for colonel, assigned to our operations division at Headquarters Marine Corps.

My boss, a Marine two-star general, called me in one day. "Look," he announced, "I'm forming a new section in the operations division.

It will be headed by a colonel. Since you've now been selected for promotion to colonel, you're going to head it up." I gave him a confused and quizzical look. It was the first I'd heard of this; and he made no mention of what exactly this new section was actually going to do. "I can't bring in new people," he continued. "We're going to have to form this new section out of our existing division assets and people. So I've identified eight people for the new section"—action officers and clerical help. He handed me a list and some other papers, and continued, "These are the people you're going to get. Here's where your office space is going to be. I've already made plans for the re-arrangement. This is your code." (Every section had codes for identifying departments and divisions, for routing staff papers, and so on.) "And this is going to be the title of your organization, Marine Air-Ground Task Force Concepts and Capabilities."

"That's sounds great, sir. What does our organization do?" I asked him.

"I'm going to get there," he said, waving me off. "This is what I want you to do: I want you to get the people together that we've identified and get settled in. Take about a week to get it all put together. Then you come back in, and I'm going to tell you in detail what this section is supposed to do and what its mission is going to be. I've been thinking about this for a long time, and I want to spend some time describing my vision and purpose for this section."

So I gathered everybody in the team, and we got started organizing ourselves and settling into our new spaces. The general was a highly regarded thinker and intellect so I was excited to be put in charge of an organization he intended to create. Here we were, a new section at Headquarters Marine Corps. We had our sign out by our door. We had our assigned code. We were ready to do business. "I can't tell you exactly what it is we're going to be doing," I told everybody. "The boss hasn't told me, but we're ready and I'm sure it will be interesting."

Everybody manned their desks and got to know each other. It was a great team so I anticipated they were selected because we would be taking on a challenging mission.

A couple of days after we hung the shingle out, we started getting what Headquarters Marine Corps calls "packages"—staff paperwork currently going through the staff process and routing. All of a sudden, packages were being staffed to me for my input and coordination. By the end of the week, my people were all busy, and masses of paperwork were coming through the pipeline. This was not just administrative stuff; it was on substance, seeking comment and input from my section's expertise and purpose. Except we didn't have those yet!

In other words, the bureaucracy had brought us into its fold.

Of course, if anybody had asked me what we were doing, I had no answer—because I had no clue. Even so, I could have continued to function. We were busy. We could have filled eight-plus hours a day. It was unbelievable. People were calling me up, asking me questions. They wanted my input. "Could you put your chop [sign-off] on this? Could you take a look at that?" . . . From what perspective? I kept asking myself. For what end? For what reason?

I had a small office that was open to the cubicles of my people. I would walk out and look them over. They were busy churning out work. We had no mission, but we were chugging along. We became consumed in the processes and activities of the bureaucracy.

Bureaucracy becomes self-fulfilling . . . a self-licking ice cream cone.

Eventually our section was truly up and running. It turned out that the job of Marine Air-Ground Task Force Concepts and Capabilities was to monitor new and emerging programs and to provide an operational perspective on them. For example, at that time we had started a new program to set up squadrons of maritime pre-position ships located at strategic points around the world; we were also setting up pre-positioned equipment sites in north Norway, where our wartime mission would take us should the Cold War turn hot; and we were developing what was then called the JVX and became the Osprey—a vertical take-off–and–landing, troop-carrying aircraft. Our boss wanted one section from the operational division to look at these programs to provide the operational concepts for their employment, a significant mission and one I truly enjoyed. Our section was real. But before we even had a clue about what we did, the bureaucracy had filled up our dance card.

That experience convinced me that you could set up a sham organization in any large bureaucracy, and your workload would come. The bureaucracy will cascade it into you.

The lesson: Leaders should not judge the value of structure and organizations by how busy they may seem. Work can often be created on its own momentum. But is it value added?

We should never confuse busywork or hard work with good work.

THE NEED FOR INTEGRATION

Today we are seeing ever-greater blending, or even the actual fusing, of organizations to meet challenges that require the integration and synergy that cooperation generates.

This is especially true of the agencies and functions of government. Resolving today's conflicts and crises requires it. The Goldwater-Nichols Act was enacted because our military services required an integrated, or joint, approach to meet today's threats more effectively and efficiently. The 9/11 Commission created the National Intelligence Directorate because commission members recognized the failure of integration among our numerous intelligence agencies. The Congressional Commission on 9/11 created the Department of Homeland Security for the same reason.

Although creating more bureaucracy is not a solution to lack of integration, it does recognize the problem. Old stovepiped organizations don't get the job done anymore.

This is not just a government problem. Today's business challenges and opportunities require integration at all levels, not just at the top.

Integration is slowly happening in government . . . faster in business.

In this new world of constant change and adaptation, the morphing, evolution, and adjustment of processes can be disruptive. Leaders must drive and oversee the adaptations and thoroughly understand the processes that form the essence of the enterprise.

This means that organizations must be learning entities. A learning organization seeks out best practices in its field; it examines itself, constantly looking for what is going right and what is going wrong; it brings in outside expertise to ensure it has the best advice and critical views; it educates and develops its leaders and members to ensure the highest level of quality in its workforce; and it is structured to rapidly implement what it learns and scrap what does not work.

TEAM BUILDING

When I joined the U.S. European Command (EUCOM) in 1990 as deputy director of operations, the command's environment was in the midst of radical change. The Soviet Union had just collapsed, the Balkans were coming apart, Eastern Europe and the former Soviet republics invited new and serious engagement, crises were breaking out in Africa, and Saddam barreled into Kuwait. The command was not used to or geared for this crisis-rich environment. To meet the demands of these emergencies, we found ourselves establishing our crisis action teams and battle staffs full time. These ad hoc organizations—originally intended to be temporary structures designed to meet short-term emergencies—were operating now 24/7.

The battle staff was a full-up, integrated, centrally located staff, with members drawn from all the functional staff elements and formed into teams or subunits to meet specific tasks. The lines of authority, tiered and layered in the day-to-day functional staff, were collapsed to gain speed and better control in processing information and making decisions during fast-breaking emergencies and crises.

The crisis action team was a smaller version of the battle staff, designed for smaller-scale and shorter-term crises.

Standing up the battle staff and crisis action team put a great strain on the EUCOM staff, since these teams came out of the hide of our classic staff structure—the stovepiped military staff dating back to the Napoleonic era and set up by functions: administration, intelligence, operations, logistics, planning, and so on. These separate and distinct functions come together only at the top, and lack integration until you reach the top. They are thus burdened with all the flaws of a traditional layered, hierarchical, block-and-wire structure.

The military had learned that you cannot fight a modern war or best handle a crisis with that structure. The crisis action team and the battle staff were therefore compact, flattened organizations that drew from each of the staff functional areas and created integrated teams, cells, boards, centers, or committees that reported directly to the command element while coordinating with and informing their respective functional staff entities. This team structure was streamlined and agile.

From our part in the Gulf War, to our operations in the Balkans, to handling several crises in Africa, to managing new relationships in Eastern Europe and the former Soviet Union, this structure gave the command and its leaders a superb means to quickly process complex and diverse information requirements, provide options, and control execution.

Because my job was to direct these organizations, I knew the strain this structure put on the providers of people and support and did my best to stand down the temporary organizations as quickly as possible. It turned out, however, that our senior leadership was reluctant to stand them down, even when the need for them had clearly passed.

"This structure is much more responsive and reactive, with greater control at our fingertips," our commander told us. He had seen the benefits of this organization during our participation in Operation Desert Storm as we supported U.S. Central Command and conducted our own military and humanitarian operations into Iraq during and after the war. He also saw its benefits during many other lesser crises during this period.

That commander reflected the new thinking that has swept through enterprises that recognize the advantages of flattened, integrated staffs in today's complex, fast-paced world. We needed the larger, more ponderous staff for day-to-day business, but it was ill suited for the new, rapid operational tempo. We flattened, teamed, and streamlined to meet those demands.

In effect, we built temporary integrated teams to overlay the traditional structure.

Creative organizations now think of themselves as seamless reservoirs of capabilities that can be shaped specifically to meet specific tasks. They are not preformed in ways that lead to mismatches and inefficiencies in applying structure to mission (like the old military staff model). Flexibility in crafting the right structure for a task is emphasized rather than force-feeding a mission into a stacked functional structure that is ill-suited for it. In the military, this shape-shifting capability is referred to as "task organization," and it requires a great deal of organizational flexibility, adaptability, and agility. This necessary mind-set encourages effective and responsive team building to meet requirements, opportunities, and challenges.

In today's environment, integrated teams representing all necessary functions of the enterprise are formed to tackle problems and pursue opportunities aimed at achieving a specific objective and are then disbanded when that effort ends. They often have a matrix relationship answering to multiple lines of authority. For this structure to work, people have to be comfortable with moving from team to team and with lines of authority that may be less direct and more divided than is traditionally the case.

At DynCorp, we formed capture teams to go after a specific contract and to work together to prepare a solid proposal that would compete well against the competition. Team members came from all parts of the company, from all the functional segments, and worked on the effort from the decision to bid on a potential contract to the hand-off to the field program manager and his team once the contract was won.

Team building isn't just a function of assigning people to a new structure. It requires careful crafting. Because this kind of integration is inevitably disruptive and comes with costs that make many people uncomfortable, many organizations have developed team training programs. They put new teams into team-building exercises and events to build cohesion and to motivate and educate members for their mission. Recognition, accountability, roles, and support are clearly laid out; and team leaders are trained in team-building skills. They're taught about dealing with friction, structuring a socialization process for new members, balancing individualism with team approaches, establishing team communications methods, recognizing exceptional achievement, ensuring total participation, and articulating and instilling common goals.

Team building is the mark of successful modern organizations. It requires serious work, skill, and understanding if it's going to be done successfully.

HELP FROM OUTSIDE

Leaders and the organizations they lead are not totally thrown on their own wits and skills as they go through the process of discovering how their organizations are structured and function or how teams are built. Just as at Quantico, skilled outside consultants can effectively map an organization and help leaders plot its parts and functions. Outside consultants normally analyze an organization better than insiders, who rarely have the objectivity to see real problems and are prone to protect business as usual. Outside consultants often see the obvious that insiders are blind to as well as the more hidden and dysfunctional "shadow" processes. They can coach teams and train team leaders in effective team building. And they can also find the critical nodes in an organization and highlight single points of dependency.

SINGLE POINTS OF DEPENDENCY

As leaders dissect their organizations, they will undoubtedly find single points of dependency or, as some call them, single points of failure. These are points in a system, process, or chain of authority where there is no backup or redundancy. If the system fails, the chief cause of the breakage often lies at one of these points. People, systems, and processes all need insurance, backup, or at least an understanding and monitoring of potential failure points. Organizations are only as strong as these points. They should be structured to provide procedures that shield the most vulnerable nodes .

A point of dependency can be inside the organization (e.g., a single individual with a unique skill or responsibility) or outside (e.g., a supplier of a critical component).

THE BUSINESS OF THE BUSINESS

Many organizations fail when they lose sight of their core competencies—what they do best and what defines them. They get sidetracked into diverse, unrelated efforts and dilute their signature capabilities, products, or skills. Though this classic cause of failure is discussed in every business school in the country, it is a greater problem today than in the past because competitive and growth pressures tempt organizations to expand and diversify more than ever before, and they are reluctant to divest themselves of nonproductive parts or to consolidate around their most productive parts.

Leaders need to maintain a laser focus on the business of the business. Failing to do that can lead to a diffusion of effort and loss of the edge that keeps an enterprise competitive. I've seen numerous businesses that have realized that they have grown too many appendages, functions, or product lines that are not related to their core skills and competencies. This realization usually happens when the need to streamline the business is driven by financial or competitiveness issues.

MODERN LEADERS KNOW THAT survival requires adaptability. They are not afraid to mold their organizations in creative and innovative ways to meet emerging challenges. They are not averse to change; and they can lead their teams through the disruptions and discomforts that come with it. They can convince teammates that the excitement and potential success far outweigh the downsides.

NINE

SPEED

General Sir John Hackett, a renowned British Army officer who served for most of the first half of the twentieth century, left in his memoirs a remarkable summing-up of his experiences during that historic period: At the dawn of the twentieth century, young officer Hackett on horseback had drawn his sword in a cavalry charge. At the end of his career as a NATO commander and commander in chief of the British Army of the Rhine, he had nuclear weapons in his command. From sword to nukes in less than half a century.

Today, equally remarkable advances in technology emerge in far less time, and they hit with far greater impact. The world moves ever faster and faster.

Cutting-edge technologies have become increasingly capable and affordable. Almost everyone on the planet has access to information technology, bringing unprecedented power to societies that don't possess much else in the way of physical or natural resources. In the eloquent words of author Thomas Friedman, technology has "flattened" the earth. It has certainly shrunk it.

Shortly after I retired from the Marine Corps, I was asked to participate in a unique project sponsored by the Defense Advanced Research Projects Agency (DARPA), a Department of Defense agency engaged in cutting-edge research into advanced technology support for the military. The project, called Command Post of the Future (CPOF), sought to develop visualization and interaction technologies aimed at radically faster situation assessment and response by combat commanders. In laymen's terms, it sought to bring state-of-the-art technology into the hands of tactical battle commanders in order to speed up their decision making, battlefield awareness, and communication of intent. The ultimate objective was to put into the hands of commanders, distributed in tactical units all over the battlefield, all the capability now resident in large command centers with huge information systems. The project went on for years, and the products that came out of it were field-tested in Iraq by innovative U.S. Army commanders.

During the course of the project, several of us old, retired warriors were asked to fight computer-simulated battles. We were placed in separate rooms and initially communicated by traditional technical means. But next to each of us was a state-of-the-art "nerd"—a young, brash, technical genius who watched us "fight," made observations, and suggested technical aids that might make our ability to manage battlefield command and control functions easier, faster, and clearer. If we liked a suggestion, our nerd churned the software, and we had the results for the next session. To us old codgers, it was truly pixel magic.

We had whiteboards. We had John Madden screens to draw on as we spoke to other commanders, and they could see our scratches. We had 3-D maps that zoomed in and out. We had contour highlighting relief maps. We had fancy displays of enemy and friendly forces that could be adjusted to focus on specific elements. And on and on. We all bonded with our geeks, who were as fascinated with our war-fighting ability as we were by their technical brilliance.

The DARPA project lasted for years. Its many other components looked at every aspect of command post requirements. I came away from it realizing, once again, that technology was rapidly evolving and would not only radically change the way we fought battles but the way we approached other fields as well.

I know highly successful businessmen and women who do most of their work away from their desks. In this globalized, fast-paced, rapidly changing environment, they have shucked the brick-and-mortar structure of offices and the ponderous processes of staffs, and replaced them with technology that allows them to conduct business on the move. They go where the action is. Their realm is cyberspace, not the physical space of corporate headquarters or operations centers. Their portable technology allows continuous contact with office and staff. They meet, are informed, plan, decide, and execute in a virtual world that replicates the old physical world with its outdated time and space boundaries.

THE VALUE OF TIME

I once asked a CEO friend what was his most valuable asset, the thing he cherished most for success. He looked at me with a slight smile. "Ask anything of me except for my time," he said.

Knowing today's technology means keeping up with it. Though today's younger leaders probably grew up with computers and video games, and are comfortable with all the latest electronic devices, they cannot become complacent. Changes, developments, and improvements come too fast for that.

It's not enough to master advancing technology. Leaders must also master its *impact.*

And that seems to move at the speed of light. Modern leaders must develop agile and adaptive minds if they hope to operate in this rapid-moving, unstructured, and confusing environment. They must quickly create order where little exists. They must make decisions in an apparent chaos that is not naturally conducive to traditional decision-making processes. Opportunities can be fleeting. Momentum can shift rapidly. Accelerated expectations can lead to immediate demands. Information can come in torrents too vast and overwhelming to be processed effectively.

And time becomes the modern leader's most valued resource.

Not just the time to process, but the time to reflect, to learn and train, and to plan for the future. Leaders now value creative time . . . a rarity in our hectic world. It must be coveted, carved out, and jealously protected.

I have coached leaders about ways to identify their most productive and creative time of day and how to block, protect, and prepare for it. Leaders need time and space to tap into their imaginations and the personal spaces that keep their batteries charged and their spirits creative. The road to success is strewn with burned-out leaders. Creative time is where the future is created and the path to it defined.

The military has an operational term for blending the present and the future: "single battle." The concept grew out of the technological advances that allowed us to see and strike farther and deeper into the battlefield. Commanders can now shape and prepare tomorrow's battle space while fighting today's battle. Their time and space horizons have so vastly increased that a series of battles—a campaign—has become a single battle fought as a logical and coherent continuum. A campaign is now conducted seamlessly and progressively. We no longer face the sequential movement that characterized the fighting of past conflicts, where event moved to event, with the conclusion of each event beginning a whole new decision process for fighting the next one.

MANAGING TIME

Wasting time is not an option for today's leaders. Time management has become as critical to success as resource and people management. Even though all other aspects of an effort are excellent, because competition—whether in business or in battle—moves and acts so fast today, lost time cannot be recovered and can cost mission success.

Time wasters have always frustrated me.

Today's most frustrating time wasters are endless meetings, video and telephone conferences, unnecessary administration tasks, and pointless e-mail exchanges. Ironically, many of these time wasters are made more attractive by the very technology that should be driving time savings, rapid decision making, and quick processing. Too many meetings drone on with no structure, agenda, or control. Too many BOGSATs (bunches of guys sitting around the table) pointlessly, endlessly, and exasperatingly address issues without accomplishing anything more than confused, watered-down groupthink.

I dread unstructured meetings. I dread video or telephone conferences that waste time grappling with the technology or the impersonal environment that these technologies necessarily produce. (It should be a given that the system is up and running and that the participants are up and running with the technology.) And I dread the hundreds of useless e-mails and paperwork that have to be dealt with each day. We need to interact. But we need to do it efficiently and effectively. We are constipating our enterprises with unstructured and undisciplined communications and interactions. Unbounded information flow and the demand for more information have consumed our attention.

The vast majority of these time wasters are aimed at meeting the top guy's need for information. As I have seen at military op center briefings and business conference rooms, these gatherings more often than not pull together people and resources from all over the organization to feed the beast of more info for the boss.

Today's successful leaders capitalize on and streamline technology so as to gain the information they need without wasting anyone's time. They value and respect the time of their subordinates as much as they value and respect their own time.

THE SPAN OF CONTROL AND THE PERSONAL TOUCH

Technology has given us the ability to reach out over great distances and control actions and people in ways that leaders even fifty years ago could never imagine. But today we have a saying: high tech, low touch. The more technology mediates our communications and contacts, the less personal our relationships.

In the late 1990s, when I commanded U.S. Central Command, my units stretched from Hawaii, to the continental United States, to the Middle East and beyond.

These great distances were never an obstacle to my command's ability to communicate. I could bring together my subordinate commands and commanders by video teleconferencing or through virtual collaborative sessions. Though many miles and many time zones separated us, we could talk to and see each other in real time. This increased my ability to influence as well as communicate.

Technology provided other advantages. Computer networking allowed us to accomplish concurrent planning with multiple staffs rather than time-consuming sequential plan development. This flattened our organization and shortened our response times.

Great stuff . . . yes. But there were drawbacks.

Video and computer networks are impersonal. I often missed the face-to-face connections, the interplay and clash of emotions, the one-on-one exchanges that can be vital to making tough decisions, and the private personal conversations that gave me insights into personalities.

While we can vastly increase the span of control, we must not do it at the cost of losing personal contact and influence.

I quickly found myself spending over 70 percent of my time on the road. I needed the personal contact in addition to the speed and convenience technology brought me. This meant picking the times and places where my personal, physical presence was most effective and those where the benefits of speed offered by technology were more effective.

We have to balance priorities. We measure that by knowing what gives us the greatest advantage and chance of success.

MOMENTUM

No organization stands still. It either grows or it slips back. Sustaining momentum is a significant challenge for today's leaders. They cannot be satisfied with just "managing things." The environment—and the fleeting opportunities and challenges it presents—is in constant flux. It must be grasped and dealt with even as the leader guides the enterprise forward.

A common mistake is to believe that the organization has "arrived" and can rest on its laurels. Organizations that expect to rest on a plateau where they can enjoy a constant, level period of achievement are setting themselves up for failure. In the past, you could revel in a success. Today you're already racing to meet the next challenge.

If you field a product that catches fire in the marketplace, you had better be planning on the new and improved version. Your competitors certainly will be, and the fickleness of the consumer could render your product yesterday's news.

Just as we can sense momentum shifting in sports events or on the battlefield, so with all other endeavors. Momentum doesn't shift slowly in today's world. Leaders have to fight hard to maintain or gain momentum against tough competitors or operating environments. It's best to assume that you are either moving up or moving down. That's why strategic planning for the future should never stop or pause.

EBB AND FLOW

There's no way an organization can maintain positive momentum forever. Momentum ebbs and flows.

We can clearly see this ebb and flow in politics. For a time—a few years, or sometimes even decades—one party will dominate, while the other will seem mired in confusion and disarray. The Democrats emerged from the Depression the "natural" ruling party until voters grew tired of Truman. Later, Ronald Reagan's presidency made Republicans the natural ruling party until the George W. Bush presidency left them in chaos. A short time ago the Democrats seemed to be doomed to even more years in the minority. Today they may be looking at many years in power, while the Republican Party desperately seeks a leader and a strategy for recovery.

Normally, governors or members of congress will emerge to take charge when a party is looking for new leaders. Some new face provides fresh hope to a party out of power as citizens weary of ineffective incumbents. So far, I don't see that process happening. The Republicans who now appear to be "leading" their party include an ultraconservative radio personality, an obscure Maryland politician who was recently elected chairman of the Republican National Committee, and a conservative intellectual who was at one time a Congressman and Speaker of the House.

Can any one of these men—Rush Limbaugh, Michael Steele, or Newt Gingrich—really be called the leader of a major American political party? Very doubtful. Maybe some young governor or member of Congress will soon take up the Republican standard and take charge.

The great prize in American politics has long been the broad electoral center where most votes lie. Successful political parties adjust to new realities and find leaders who excite both the center and their own party's base on the left or on the right. By the same token, their formerly successful opposition fails to maintain the trust and confidence of the voters at the center, and the inevitable ebb and flow repeats. This is healthy. It prevents parties from becoming stale and over-accustomed to power. Change and competition make for better organizations. The bastards get voted out.

Our free market economy is founded on a similar process. An organization that loses its competitive edge or that becomes weak or otherwise flawed will either get its act together and return to health or it will die.

The automobile industry is already a classic example of this grim but useful evolutionary process. An asteroid hit the industry decades ago in the form of superior foreign competitors who made American automakers' business and labor practices seem outmoded. Are our American dinosaurs too big and essential to our economy to fail? The debate rages: Should the government (which is to say you and me) try to save GM and Chrysler, the weakest of the industry's American dinosaurs . . . especially after their sorry leadership demonstrated their own failure to understand that their competitors were more attentive to market demands and that their own assumptions about customer loyalty were dead wrong? The fiasco that attended their appearance at public Congressional hearings in late 2008 confirmed everyone's worst fears about the industry's corporate leadership. The testifying CEOs—General Motors CEO Richard Wagoner, Ford CEO Alan Mulally, and Chrysler CEO Robert Nardelli—came across as stereotypical, out of touch, overcompensated crybabies in search of a handout. We, and our Congressional representatives, wanted to hear a sound recovery strategy, a clear admission of fault, and a commitment to change. We didn't get it.

Organizations have to periodically reinvent themselves and revitalize their leadership. It's true in politics, business, and all other endeavors.

MASTERING TECHNOLOGY

Contrast the candidates for the presidency in 2008. One had mastered the Internet; the other hadn't. John McCain proudly claimed that he couldn't and didn't do e-mail. The other, Barack Obama, ran the first twenty-first-century campaign. He masterfully used the Internet to organize, mobilize, and rally over 2 million volunteers; to communicate his message; and to gain an overwhelming advantage in funding. His use of the Internet effectively connected his key constituencies of young people and highly educated people, and gained him a tremendous advantage and momentum from the early primaries through to the presidential campaign and election.

In one of his campaign promises, Obama pledged to ensure broadband access to all Americans. He clearly understands the age we live in. Yesterday, the emerging technologies were the telephone, radio, and TV. Today's emerging technology is the Internet. Who knows what tomorrow will bring—holographic sessions in your living room or office?

COMPETITION FOR TIME

Competition for time comes into play everywhere, and in every field of endeavor—economics, politics, warfare, diplomacy . . . a competition that is greatly complicated because different cultures and nations have different perspectives on time and how to use it.

The Chinese, for example, take a long view of time. Because they have been in the civilization business for millennia and expect to be in business for many more millennia, they tend to believe that long spans of time favor them. They rarely make sudden, impulsive moves. They plan ahead. Their changes are always incremental. They expect to prevail, but they don't feel urgency to prevail tomorrow.

Our Western society looks at a shorter time horizon, and we tend to operate a lot faster than the majority of our enemies or those who compete with us. That normally means that if we are going to prevail—in war or in business or wherever—we have to prevail in a shorter period of time than they do.

Our enemies will therefore try to come at us with an asymmetric approach that aims to draw us out over a longer period of time. I saw this in Vietnam. The enemy could suffer defeat after defeat but slowly regroup and return. His sense of time opposed our will to sustain the conflict.

Al Qaeda and other terrorist groups try to take a long perspective: "Beat us up now, we'll just go into hiding until you go away. We have all the time in the world. You don't. You can't sustain the will to be here. We can nickel and dime you, and eventually we'll wear you down."

They try to turn us into the helpless giant, stumbling and bludgeoning ineffectively with all our high-tech toys.

We don't have to fall into that hole.

Instead, we can *use* our speed to beat them.

How?

We make their long view irrelevant. We make relevant changes happen so fast that their longer approach collapses in confusion, chaos, and irrelevance.

In Aesop's fables, the tortoise beat the hare. The hare ran out of steam. He got distracted. He didn't know how to use time. His ego and his arrogance got in the way.

But if the hare had used his time effectively and stayed focused, there was no way the tortoise's determination, plodding, and steady pace would have beaten him to the finish.

We have to take the advantage of time away from our enemies and our competitors. If I act effectively and create a hostile environment for you faster than you can create a hostile environment for me, time becomes a disadvantage to you.

So far we've spent perhaps a trillion dollars over six years in Iraq.

What if we had initially gone into Iraq with a very different program: "We're going to fix this problem our way—fast, sharp, and well. We're going to turn Iraq over in two years. We understand the scope of the problem. We've made a thorough analysis. We're going to spend a trillion dollars. We're going to put 400,000 troops in there. We're going to launch a vast economic development program—like the Marshall Plan. We're going to freeze the security situation . . . and overwhelm it. We're going to seal the borders. We're going to work with the people."

In other words, with a better understanding of the situation (with a better assessment of the environment), we would have taken all the expenditures of resources and manpower over six-plus years and focused them into two or less. Those who thought they were going to beat us over the long haul might have found themselves overwhelmed.

That would have been real shock and awe.

GLOBAL TIME

The old excuse for taking a nice comforting drink earlier than is fashionably proper has always been "Well, it's five o'clock somewhere in the world." We all now live by that clock . . . though not, one hopes, the practice.

We are now on a global clock with a 24/7 workday. Our flat and shrunken world requires 24/7 attention and decision making. I have never been part of an organization that could sleep. Naturally the military couldn't, with its global commitments and presence, nor could the diplomatic world I found myself in, nor the large corporations I was part of. But even the relatively small business enterprises I've been associated with have to master the global clock. Things just can't wait till morning. The demands put on resources and leadership further eat up the time required for people to stay ahead of the game and to react to opportunities and challenges.

STATE OF THE ART

On a recent visit to I Marine Expeditionary Force (I MEF), the Marine operational command on our West Coast, I was given a firsthand look at what is called the Infantry Immersion Center. It was set up in a huge, previously abandoned tomato canning factory located on the edge of Camp Pendleton, California.

Inside the facility, the Marines had created a large, seemingly living Iraqi neighborhood . . . with realistic sights, sounds, and smells.

Live Iraqi role players had been hired to enact situations the Marines would, and had, experienced in Iraq. Squads of Marines went through various realistic scenarios like those they would face in their upcoming tours of duty in Iraq. Routine events and issues they would confront were thrown at them, along with nonroutine events, such as IED explosions, terrorist attacks, and the handling of very real-looking casualties. (Some of the Iraqi American role players were actual amputees from the war.)

The scenarios were designed to focus on moral, ethical, and legal decision making; put realistic stress on the Marines and the young leaders; and increase their confidence, team building, and combat effectiveness. They were mentored and accompanied through these drills by small-unit leaders who had faced these same situations in real life. They critiqued actions and decisions as well as offered advice.

What was unique and innovative about this training complex was the way technology had been blended into the mix. A video capture system recorded each squad's every action for use in debriefs and critiques. Interactive holographic displays were added to the "real" environment to create when-to-shoot situations; and the holographic video characters had been programmed with optional reactions based on the decisions made and the effectiveness of the shots on the targets: A "wounded" terrorist, for example, would act differently from one who'd received a lethal shot. High-fidelity sensory effects were produced by technology that generated sights, smells, and sounds so realistic that those who had been in Iraq reacted as if they were back on those streets once again.

This innovative blending of physical and technical reality created a nearly real world. The time needed to train the units was greatly reduced, the number of training situations and evolutions in that time were vastly increased, and the cost to create the "reality" desired was minimized.

Technology can buy time and efficiency. But it has to be masterfully managed to ensure we don't become slaves to it.

TEN

KNOWLEDGE

Back when I was a young second lieutenant platoon commander, I was greatly impressed by my company commander, an aggressive, at times abrasive guy, not very much liked by the senior leadership; yet he clearly knew what a captain had to know to do his job—a lot more, it always seemed, than the officers above him. Even if they didn't particularly like him, probably because of his superior knowledge, they always showed him respect . . . even fear. In meetings, everyone deferred to him . . . went silent once he started talking. He had such a forceful presence that no one challenged or questioned him.

Though he was tough and often difficult (he didn't tolerate fools), I liked him and got along well with him; and he always took time to mentor and teach me. One day in his office, I asked him why he had such a strong effect on other people. He gestured toward a set of bookcases against the walls. "See those books and manuals?" he asked, smiling. "I know just about everything in them. I study my profession and pride myself on my knowledge. Those who don't do that are always intimidated by those who know, learn, and think."

That impressed me, but more than that, it nurtured my curiosity and hunger to study my calling in the profession of arms. It became clear to me early on that the greatest respect was always paid to those who were regarded as the most professionally competent and knowledgeable.

In the early 1970s, I ran a school for infantry units that included a course for NCOs, young corporals and sergeants who had all seen combat in Vietnam. During the leadership phase of the course, I would ask them to identify the single top leadership quality they wanted in their platoon commander. "We want him to know his stuff" over 98 percent of them answered. (They didn't say "stuff"; they were Marines.)

Today's young people give me a very different answer when I ask that question in my classes and leadership sessions. Because they have never been in trying leadership situations like combat or managing crises, their top leadership qualities tend to be softer: "caring for people" or "honesty and truthfulness." Though there's nothing wrong with those qualities (I far prefer leaders who are caring, honest, and truthful), the difference is striking between what the young folks perceive they need and what the old dogs want. The old dogs have been through tough times; they want, first and foremost, a leader who knows his "stuff" and will get them through the rough patches. They know from experience that a leader who is competent but not nice is better than a leader who is nice but not competent.

My curiosity and hunger for knowledge has stayed with me throughout my life. And in today's trying times, I've come to realize that true leadership calls for even more than professional competence.

In recent years, I have run international operations for several companies and provided consulting services for several others that aimed to increase their international presence. These experiences have taught me the value of deep and broad knowledge of the arena where we do business. We have to be familiar with how people live, think, feel, and conduct themselves. We have to appreciate their richness, not just the ways they differ from us. To arrive anywhere in the world armed only with a narrow knowledge of our own business is not enough. More broadly knowledgeable competitors will command far greater local respect and leave us in their dust.

My military experiences taught me a similar lesson: Out there in the world of today, military competence is not enough to get even the military job done.

When I was commander in chief of U.S. Central Command, my mission and tasks required solid knowledge of global economics, international trade, media relations, energy issues, environmental is-

sues, cultural issues, political issues, and human rights and humanitarian issues as well as security and military issues. There no longer is
a pure military command. Military decisions are tightly woven into a
mix of political, economic, cultural, and other factors. Leading strategic organizations—military, government, business, or others—now
requires the broadest possible education and knowledge base. The
knowledge I required did not—it could not—come only from reading and study. I had to talk to experts in every field and see firsthand
the physical components of what I needed to know. I made sure I
went out to meet and spend time with local people and to plunge into
their customs and traditions. The pleasures of the plunge were real,
yet I could not have done my job if I had not made the effort to get
away from what could have become a heavily insulated military cocoon and experience what was going on beyond it.

In addition to my military duties as commander of CENTCOM,
over the years I have been sent by our government on eight peace mediation and diplomatic missions, and I have participated in a number
of environmental studies and programs. Military expertise alone
would have gotten me nowhere on these missions. I needed not only
to study the issues but to "see" the issues. I had to be on the ground
and in the environment of contesting parties.

I went to Sumatra to meet with the Free Aceh Movement; I went to
Mindanao to meet with the Moro Islamic Liberation Front; I went
to the West Bank and Gaza to meet with the Palestinian Authority. I
witnessed the effects of global warming on melting glaciers and talked
to scientists with competing views.

A lot of responsibility came with these assignments; poking my nose
into areas not traditionally military was vital. Not everyone approved.

In her controversial book, *The Mission: Waging War and Keeping
Peace with America's Military, Washington Post* reporter Dana Priest
suggests that America's role in the world of today parallels Rome's in
the ancient world. In her view, our actual effect in the world is very
like an empire, and combatant commanders (those who command
our regional unified commands, such as CENTCOM) have become
the present-day incarnations of Roman proconsuls. Her provocative

ideas raised quite a ruckus: Many thoughtful people felt that by involving ourselves in broader nonmilitary issues, military commanders had exceeded our authority and scope of responsibility. We were out of our lane. Other thoughtful people disagreed. In their view, military commanders were filling voids that had to be filled and no one else was filling. Other government agencies have not been given the resources, manpower, and authority necessary to contribute to the engagement and reconstruction efforts needed to protect our interests around the world.

In the aftermath of the Iraq and Afghanistan invasions, there is growing acknowledgment of the need to find better ways to fill the voids that have to be filled, and both Congress and the current administration seem committed to doing that.

But filling them is not just a matter of providing nonmilitary agencies with greatly improved capabilities; it also requires leadership that knows how to integrate all the necessary functions at every level.

In my view, the new and more powerful role of combatant commanders is a sign that we have moved to a new age in which narrow ranges of authority and expertise can no longer be effective. When we interact with other nations, societies, or cultures, the complex intersection and overlap of societal functions and institutions no longer permit specialization.

THE FUTURE OF KNOWLEDGE

Because intellectual assets are the underpinning of a knowledge-based economy, investment in human capital and research and development is fundamental to continued growth. For policymakers, this requires greater attention to educating and training children and adults. U.S. corporations now operate globally, competing with corporations based in other countries for skilled knowledge workers. Experts predict that the shortage of skilled knowledge workers globally will only grow more critical and jeopardize U.S. economic growth and competitiveness.

Both the U.S. government and the private sector are experiencing a shortage of workers with the cultural understanding and skills, including language skills, needed to work in the global environment.

These words come from the U.S. Government Accountability Office's 2007 report, "Forces That Will Shape America's Future."

During my international business experiences, I have seen too many senior executives who cannot do business effectively in a global environment; their education, interests, and experience have evolved too narrowly. To far more sophisticated global executives, they are boring and incomplete. If we want to compete and succeed, we must attain broader knowledge.

In business, there is a term for those whose knowledge is only narrow and technical. They are called "tall, thin people." We require now a far broader knowledge—like a liberal arts education. Technical expertise is not enough; we need renaissance men and women.

An engineering education is very good and useful, but that kind of specialized knowledge becomes less and less good and useful the higher you rise as an executive. The same is true in the military: An artillery officer rises to become a four-star general. What good is an expert artillery specialist at that level if that is all he has going for him? Rising young officers have to branch out into many other areas—including, but far from limited to, more holistic knowledge of the total military spectrum. They also have to understand economics, politics, diplomacy, and other cultures. You can no longer be successful by mastering a very narrow field.

The day and age of the boss who puts his nose to the grindstone and is totally focused on the workings of his business and nothing else is over.

The most progressive companies have long been aware of the need for this broad knowledge. I was recently asked by Exxon-Mobil to talk to a gathering of executives about the Middle East and its culture and dynamics. In the past, companies may not have devoted attention to such things: "What do I care? I find oil, pump it, and that's it. It doesn't matter where it comes from." No longer. They now feel it's vitally important for their senior leadership to understand the cultures of the countries where they operate, what's happening out there, and where they may be headed. I was impressed by the investment made in educating their personnel in these areas and the enthusiasm their people displayed.

The Department of Defense has also recognized this reality. In 2008, DOD formally activated a new regional military command (like CENTCOM or EUCOM) called the African Command (AFRICOM). Unlike the other regional command structures, AFRICOM will experiment with an integrated staff composed of representatives from government agencies other than DOD. This new structure recognizes that diplomatic, informational, military, and economic activities, and all the other elements of our power, can't be exercised in isolation. The U.S. Southern Command, which deals with our security interests in Central and South America, has achieved highly effective and cutting-edge organizational and integration restructuring in this same mode. Their commander, Admiral Jim Stravidis, is a brilliant leader with foresight, education, and vision who intuitively grasps the integrated capabilities needed to operate a strategic organization today.

Leading an organization with complex, integrated functions requires exceptionally broad knowledge, education, and experience.

How do we broaden our knowledge?

We can start by nurturing and improving our own curiosity. And by asking ourselves questions like:

Where do I gather my information?
How do I do it?
How do I expand my knowledge level?
How do I expand my interest level?
How do I expand my experiences?

Answering these questions has more to do with self-education and drive than anything else. Although many institutions have invested in broadening opportunities for education and experience, anyone aspiring to be a successful twenty-first-century leader must look after his or her own development. This requires drive, risk, curiosity, and commitment.

But it takes more than just increasing your knowledge and gaining experience. You have to know what to do with your knowledge and experience, how to think about what you know, and how it applies to what you do.

HOW TO THINK

Today we live in an oversimplified, attention-deficit, sound-bite, bumper-sticker society. We tend to look at surfaces and not depths. When we ask questions about a problem or issue, we want simple and linear answers and solutions.

Too many leaders make snap judgments in the misguided conviction that an innate or instinctive ability to make good decisions is wired into their makeup . . . or else that God has given that ability to them. They work on hunches, intuitions, instinct, or inspiration, and then immediately launch into solutions or courses of action without fully understanding what they face or the best way to handle it. Intuition and inspiration are valuable and useful, but only when they spring out of long and deeply examined experience. Otherwise, they are no more reliable than magic.

Reality doesn't work that way.

The world is made out of systems; few of them are simple. On the contrary, any systems we have to understand are growing ever more complex, intricate, and fast-morphing, even as demands grow ever more pressing and available time grows shorter. In spite of these very real limits, we need to take time to analyze and understand. As the old saying goes, "If you want it bad, you'll get it bad."

Since we cannot begin to plumb all the depths of the myriad issues that confront our enterprise, our skills must include knowing how to acquire relevant information, analyze it, and turn it into insight. This ability leads to developing a true and viable vision for our future direction. And we need to know how to triage information—how not to be trapped into acquiring knowledge we don't need and can't use.

To put this another way, thinking effectively has three modes: systems thinking, critical thinking, and creative thinking. These modes of thinking are certainly not new; but the emphasis that forward-looking institutions and organizations put on them is.

Systems thinking is the ability to see deeply into the complex, interconnected systems that make up our environment.

Critical thinking is the ability to analyze these systems and, through synthesis, build our understanding of them.

Creative thinking is the ability to innovate and imagine practical solutions and new paths based on our analysis and synthesis.

A great modern leader masters and consistently demonstrates each of these modes and fuses them into a single process as he approaches every problem or decision.

We have to appreciate the complexity of the system before we can begin to analyze it. And then we begin our analysis by breaking the system down into its component parts. Synthesis brings the parts back together in a way that frames the system and allows us to understand it. Creative thinking leads us toward a vision of how to survive, thrive, and prosper in that environment.

I have seen excellent critical or analytical thinkers who can clearly define a problem and define its structure but cannot creatively come up with solutions. I have also seen creative thinkers who are not bound by conventional thinking and who can pull ideas out of the box every minute but cannot think in a systems or critical way to refine or sharpen their ideas to make them more relevant and executable.

WHAT'S THE PROBLEM?

Analysis begins with a *clear* answer to that question.

Too often in my military and business experience, I've watched people rush to provide solutions to problems when we were not even sure what the problems were. That's the principal cause of bad decisions. It's a natural tendency . . . *and* a big component in the American character. American leaders—military, business, academic, political—will never admit they don't understand anything. We tend to leap to provide answers or solutions to any question or problem, even if we don't fully understand it.

Problems erupt. Someone runs in the boss's door: "Sir! We've got a nasty situation!"

The boss shouts: "Get everybody together!"

All the top officers or executives rush in and sit around the conference table.

The boss is in a panic. "Here's the problem." He lays out the symptoms. Then he goes around the table asking everybody to shoot out ideas. "Joe, what do you think? What can we do?" . . . "Sam, what do you think? What can we do?"

And Joe and Sam and everybody else throw out solutions.

No!

Somebody's got to break in and say: "Stop! Stop! Everybody's throwing out ideas and solutions. But nobody truly understands the problem. We just see symptoms and shoot from the hip. Before we go any further, we've got to define the problem."

That's the first act of right thinking: *Define the problem. What are we facing?*

Defining the problem most often yields these possible results:

We separate the symptoms from the core causes.
We may find that the problem is not as bad as we thought, or it may be worse.
We may find that it's different from what we thought.
We may find that it has component parts that have to be broken down into multiple solution sets before we can reach the ultimate conclusion.

We have to ask the right questions. It's not the answer, it's the question that you have to pay attention to. The right answer may or may not come. But absent the right questions, chances are it will never come.

I'm driving along and my engine dies. I pull over and ask myself, "What am I going to do?" I think of possibilities: Call a mechanic. Call a tow. Check the gas. Do this. Do that. But then I say to myself, "Stop, wait a minute. Let's look at exactly what's going on with my car. Let's lift the hood and take a look at the engine before I do anything else." I look under the hood and see that something got unplugged. I plug it back in, and the engine starts. . . . Or maybe the gauge had broken and I didn't know I'd run out of gas.

To sum up: Before we act on the problem, we have to define the problem.

THINKING STYLES

There's no single right approach to systems, critical, and creative thinking.

During the recent presidential election campaign, I was asked by several candidates from both parties to provide my views on a number of issues, including the Middle East, the military, and the wars in Iraq and Afghanistan. The candidates all processed information in their own ways.

Some of them would bone up on the issues, study all the reports and briefs, bring in experts with differing views, and then debate them. These debates were not adversarial; the leaders simply wanted to challenge and be challenged, and in that way sharpen and refine their understanding.

Other candidates didn't bury themselves in reports and written briefs. They wanted to listen to the issues. They wanted multiple oral briefs and differing views, which they would then process internally on their own.

Others learned from scenarios and games. For example, if they wanted to understand energy issues, they would have their staffs create an "energy scenario." Say, a security crisis in the Persian Gulf threatens the supply of oil and natural gas. People will come in and role-play. Somebody plays the secretary of defense. Another plays the secretary of energy. Another plays the chairman of the Joint Chiefs. Another plays the commander of CENTCOM. And so on. In the con-

text of the scenario, the leader is fed expertise, and he makes decisions. Afterward, the experts critique them.

Every leader has to find his own thinking style, his own way of effectively processing information. There's no one way to do it. We can
teach people analytical thinking, systems thinking, and creative thinking. But they then have to adopt a process that works best for them.

UNDERSTANDING EXPERIENCE

Experience comes every waking second, but only some of it is valuable. The most valuable experiences shine in our memory and cast
light on one another. The older experiences teach ever more powerful
lessons after contact with the more recent ones. And vice versa.

I still draw lessons from my time in Vietnam as an adviser. Yet I
couldn't appreciate and use these rich leadership and other experiences
until education, understanding, and other leadership experiences and
lessons made them come alive to provide powerful *new* lessons.

A group from a military technology support lab recently asked
me to help them develop methods and technology supports to train
young Marines and soldiers for a greater "sense of the firefight"—a
term I used in my 2004 book, *Battle Ready,* to describe how—after
long combat experience—I became more aware and knowledgeable
of a combat situation. The group wanted to know how I had learned
to discriminate, process, and synthesize sensual clues during a swiftly
flowing and chaotic firefight and then make good tactical decisions
based on my sense.

In the beginning of my Vietnam tour, I couldn't tell the difference
between an AK–47 firing and an M–16; but after eleven months, I
could. I began to have what the Germans call a "fingertip sense of the
firefight." I could read it, and my reading was usually right.

"What were your cues?" the group members asked me. "Acoustic?
Visual? Other senses, like smell? And how did you put them together?"

"The cues were primarily acoustic," I told them, "but there were
also visual cues; and even smell." I could tell, as time went on, the

distinctive reports of different weapons systems, the locations of weapons, the maneuvering of troops, and so on.

Some business executives I've known have a similarly keen sixth-sense ability to look at a deal or a contract and tease out problems or issues other, less-experienced people miss. When pushed on how they do it, they always go back to their tremendous breadth of experience, coupled with the increased knowledge gained from the analytic processing of their experiences.

It's great to see it all, but we also have to process it all.

We are not on our own as we work to understand our experiences. Useful tools are available to help us do that.

When I need to analyze a knotty recent event or a situation that's still evolving, I like to run it through the filters of a mentor, counselor, or someone else with deep experience whom I respect. The old sergeant helps the young corporal understand the squad firefight he just went through. He tells him what he did right or wrong and how to put it into context.

When I go to some trusted mentor for guidance, I will describe the experience in detail: "Look, this is what I went through. I did this. They did that." As I entered the business world after retiring from the military, I sought out several experienced advisers in the fields I was entering. I had the education I needed (a bachelor's and a master's degree in business), but I knew the value of the experience that I lacked . . . more directly, the value of relevant analyzed and examined experience. The mentor or adviser and I talk about it. He asks questions, makes comments, adds input, gives his personal angle on the experience, all aimed at helping me understand it.

THE VALUE OF HISTORY

I also examine experiences under the light of other experiences—either my own past experiences or those from history that I glean through reading and study.

I've learned to use the lessons of the past but not to trust them blindly.

Many times I've worked through a problem or a decision process that produced good results. The success felt good: "Man, I got it right this time. I know how to do it. The next time I'm in this kind of situation, I know what to do." But then months—or more likely years—later, I reach another experience level that opens a much clearer window, and I realize that what I did the first time only works in that particular situation. It doesn't carry over. The situation may look the same on the surface, but the decision I have to make requires a very different option, approach, or angle.

I not only examine and reexamine my own experiences, I study history. And as a military man, I study past battles and the more abstract principles and theories of warfare and combat. Ever since mankind began, forces have been engaging each other in battle. Considerable human intelligence has gone into trying to understand why and how we do that. Anyone who wishes to understand warfare and combat must study the best thinking on it.

The various tools and lenses for analyzing experience aren't used in isolation from one another. We have to bring them together.

Let's say that the Marine Corps Command and Staff College has asked me to run a war game exercise. There will be assigned readings that describe scenarios and situations much like what would be experienced in the game. I might bring in a retired general who once fought in a campaign similar to the one we'd be gaming. (I'm occasionally asked to play this role.) He would talk to me about his campaign and walk through the gaming situation with me, commenting on what he sees through the filter of his own experience. I would question him and get his guidance. I'd meanwhile do research into other historical campaigns and look back over my own personal experience . . . maybe something I did in Iraq, Somalia, or Vietnam will have relevance. I'll throw that into the mix too. And of course, long before this particular exercise, my professional education has spotlighted the theory and practice that I need for this situation. Then I bring all those together when I do the exercise.

I was recently asked by the commander of the Joint Forces Command (where much of our joint strategy, concepts, and doctrine are produced) to moderate a panel of distinguished historians looking at how successful grand strategic visions were produced in the past. The commander, General Jim Mattis, is one of our military's best thinkers. And it made a lot of sense to him to work through a historical analysis—gaining insights from the past that may have application for the future—before plunging into today's requirement for a strategic design.

Half a dozen historians presented the approaches to grand strategy of empires and nations from the Romans to the United States after World War II. The descriptions of what, why, and how strategies were developed and implemented were brilliantly insightful. Through this historical analysis, General Mattis built a foundation of understanding for his and his command's thoughts about our future strategy; the lessons he ticked off from his copious notes were impressive.

WHAT'S THE BEST TOOL for teaching and learning—lectures, seminars, or case studies?

Law schools and business schools value case studies; and in my experience teaching ethics and foreign policy, I have come to the same conclusion. The method has a drawback, however. If you do it properly, you can effectively engage only a limited number of students. If there are too many, students won't have enough time to fully develop and present their assigned cases.

Successful businesses have also come to recognize the value of these methods and include them in leader training and off-sites for leader reflection and development.

STREET CRED

Equally essential to effective leadership is street credibility and street smarts.

The old sergeant who was there when the bullets were flying, the project manager who has run numerous field operations, the experienced construction site foreman are all invaluable. They bring the practioner's view to decision making and planning. Having seen the fog and friction on the ground, they offer a level of granularity and detail necessary for thoroughly knowledgeable input: street smarts.

Leaders who possess these skills enjoy within their field or professional community a special reputation for superior performance and long-term consistency that mark them as true experts: street cred.

Street cred and street smarts—in the military our term is "situational awareness" (SA)—require the innate curiosity to delve into, understand, clearly articulate, and quickly tie together the critical details gleaned from experience that are necessary for effective decision making.

A pilot who has hundreds of flying hours, good developed instincts, a real sense of what goes on around him, and can process in split seconds numerous disparate events has high SA. Those who have honed these flying skills to that level often become valued instructors.

KNOWLEDGE: TODAY'S HOT COMMODITY

Advances in technology come blindingly fast. Where it once took twenty years to develop, field, and reap the benefits of a new technology, it is now common to see a new technology developed, fielded, exploited, and obsolescent in that many months.

It's not enough to develop exciting new technologies; the far greater challenge is to be innovative in their applications. No new technologies went into iPods and iPhones.

Knowledge is no less a product than everything made in factories.

We exited the Industrial Age long ago. We now live and work in a knowledge-based economy where human capital has become far more important than physical capital. Marketing knowledge is the hot new business. It requires bright and innovative leadership and smart workers.

Our nation now competes with a growing number of societies that grasp the value of brains over brawn (industrial might).

To stay competitive, organizations must now focus first on bringing in smart recruits who hunger for knowledge and then on developing and training them as far as they can be developed and trained. Incentives given to those who seek further education and training are investments in a more competitive force.

A LEADER WHO WISHES to make it in today's challenging world has to know more. He also has to know how to understand and use what he knows. If learning is a drudgery, you won't get where you need to go. Organizations want leaders with the intellect, talent, passion for learning, curiosity, and open minds that make them able to operate successfully in a highly competitive and complex environment and to set the vision and course for the future. In the words of Sergeant Stryker (John Wayne's role in the *Sands of Iwo Jima*), "Life is tough, but it's tougher if you're stupid."

ELEVEN

COMMUNICATION

When Cicero spoke, people marveled. When Caesar spoke, people marched.

Cato the Younger

Words are actions. They move people to action. They cause change. Or stop it. This is true of written words, spoken words, and images on screens.

Roman politician Cato the Younger got it right two millennia ago. When great leaders speak, people march.

Lou Cannon, a *Washington Post* White House correspondent and the author of several books on Ronald Reagan, wrote extensively about the reasons why President Reagan was revered as the "Great Communicator." According to Cannon, the president naturally connected to people and knew his audience. His public words were always evocative, simple, and mainstream . . . filled with a loving sense of country and liberally spiced with folksy anecdotes that people could relate to. His message was, more often than not, directed toward the future and always optimistic; he seemed to stand for something.

It would be easy to chalk Reagan's communicating genius up to acting skills, and certainly that training and experience were valuable assets. But it was more than that. As Cannon says, "America was inside him." And that came across. Most Americans felt secure with him. He was like a father to us, in charge and in control. Everything would be okay.

Reagan was the external and internal face of our country. Much like FDR, we looked up to his leadership in trying times, and we felt more confident and hopeful because of his leadership—a confidence built in no small part on his charisma and exceptional ability to communicate his message. Like FDR, Kennedy, Lincoln, and other great presidents, Reagan seemed to enjoy the act of communicating. He was America.

Contrast that with the parade of CEOs we have recently seen testifying before congressional committees. Do they radiate confidence? Do they seem to enjoy communicating? Do they personify their organizations? Most of the enterprises they lead face dire crises. Their stakeholders need them to attack these crises. Are the CEOs leading the attack? Those watching and questioning are looking for CEOs to stand accountable, accept responsibility, identify with their enterprise, and reassure the public. Do any of these qualities emerge?

In their greatest moment of challenge as leaders, only a few come across as we hope and expect. The few who do live up to expectations are a rare breed who understand that today's leader must be open, public, and communicative. He must be the face of his enterprise and represent it fully and positively—in good times and in bad.

SHORTLY AFTER I TOOK command of U.S. Central Command, the foreign minister of Qatar, Sheikh Hamad bin Jassim Al Thani, asked me to agree to be interviewed by Al Jazeera television. I balked. It was well understood that Al Jazeera wasn't friendly to America or Americans, and up to that time we had kept a low profile in the region, for good reason.

"Whether the interview is friendly or not," Sheikh Hamad told me, "it's crucial to put a human face on the American military in our region. If you don't," he continued, "you'll leave the communication of your image to those who will present it in a bad light. There's great skepticism about your reasons for being here. It's important for you to respond to these doubts; but even more important, you have to show who you really are."

I reluctantly agreed to several interviews. Though they weren't easy, the questions and follow-ups were good and balanced. In one interview, for example, I was asked about how we accounted for possible collateral damage and the "moral" aspects of our actions in operational planning. This excellent question allowed me to describe the painstaking measures and risks we took to ensure civilian safety and respect for religious and historical sites. I described how we strictly adhered to the tenets of Just War doctrine and how our legal staff ensured compliance. I also described how our rules of engagement were crafted and structured, and even our rationale for assigning chaplains to our units. They were direct moral representatives, giving moral guidance to our men and women during the stress of combat.

Later feedback indicates that my Al Jazeera interviews succeeded in showing America in a positive light. The minister's savvy advice about "putting a human face" on our military leadership was right on.

I did not regret the experience. It made me realize that you can't let others define you or your organization. The leader must step forward and give his organization an honest and accurate personal presence. The days of leading by decree and from the sanctuary of an oak-paneled office are over.

I'VE SERVED ON OVER a dozen advisory boards and boards of directors and heard scores of presentations by CEOs and company presidents in hundreds of board and committee meetings.

They "present" their enterprises to their stakeholders in many ways.

A few grab me with crisp, insightful descriptions, balancing detailed data with vividly articulated and confidence-inspiring statements of vision and direction. They have a visible passion for leading their enterprise to success.

Many others lose me, with vague, rambling, disconnected pitches, overloaded with barely coherent, boring detail.

When addressing their people, many leaders today make their presentations in free and open town hall–style meetings, where questions and comments are welcomed and expected. This format gives the led a chance to take a closer measure of the guy or gal at the top, to get answers about burning issues, or to air the good and the bad as seen from the bottom. I've seen bosses who enjoy the interaction and thrive in this format. They come across as caring, confident, sincere, and on top of things. I've seen others who are more anxious and uncomfortable engaging in public interaction. They turn people off.

The ability of leaders to effectively communicate the nature, quality, and future of their enterprise has enormous impact on stakeholder confidence. It is the single most important factor in generating that trust.

A CEO acquaintance of mine inspired investor commitment based solely on his personal reputation and force of personality. When I first met him, investors were lining up to put millions into a new enterprise he was launching; few of them seemed to care about financial or other business details.

I asked him how he had gained their faith.

"I have a history with these investors," he told me. "I've earned their trust. Today my word is good enough for them."

When I asked several of his investors the same question, they gave me the same answer. Of course he delivered (you have to perform, and your performance has to be tested and measured), but he also projected the confidence and commitment they sought in someone they were trusting with their cash. They liked the cut of the man.

The power of performance obviously inspires others and gains trust, confidence, and commitment. But these can die on the vine unless the leader honestly communicates the qualities that have produced and will continue to produce successful performance.

We recently watched our former president, secretary of the Treasury, and other government officials try to explain to Congress and the American people why financial, industrial, and other institutions had to be rescued with a gigantic, multi-hundred-billion-dollar federal bailout.

After their pitch, few members of Congress—and few of us—understood the complex crisis they were trying to explain and resolve.

"Is a bailout the right answer? Will it work?"

In the end, Congress supported their proposals, though without much confidence in either the necessity for a rescue or their ability to deliver the fix they were promising. It was a struggle. We don't like taxpayer money bailing out Wall Street or failed businesses. But Congress could not stomach the potential collapse of the nation's financial system.

We saw the chief executives of the three major U.S. car manufacturers sent packing after their first attempt to get a bailout from Congress. They not only failed to make their case effectively at a critical moment, they left a terrible impression—and company image—after they arrived in corporate jets and seemed blind to the effects generated by their excessive pay packages.

IF THEY HAVE THE credibility and the skills necessary to convince the skeptical, great communicators can sell ideas, plans, or programs to audiences disinclined to accept them. Great leaders make people march. George Marshall sold to a Congress dominated by the opposition party and to the leery American people his initially deeply unpopular plan to invest a vast portion of our national treasure in reconstructing Europe and Japan—even including our former enemies. It took over eighty speeches all over the country and countless face-to-face meetings with influential and powerful people, but he pulled it off. A George Marshall could do that.

Whatever he or she may be called—general, chief executive officer, head coach, president, bishop, queen—the leader personifies the institution. They are the face the enterprise puts before the world.

They embody the enterprise. Their personality and character define its personality and character.

People inside and outside an institution look to its leaders for clear guidance; they expect leaders to communicate the mission, character, and vision of the enterprise to itself and to the world.

DEVELOPING COMMUNICATORS

In this day and age, organizations invest a great deal to develop leaders into articulate spokesmen for their enterprise.

Consulting and training outfits provide advice and specialized training. Nothing is overlooked—physical appearance, clothing, mannerisms, gestures, wording, style . . . even audience analysis. Trainees are put through stressful sessions and scenarios simulating tough situations: They deliver messages people don't want to hear; they handle a crisis before an aggressive media or angry constituency; they pitch a daring, risky, but potentially hugely profitable new product.

There is no substitute for doing it. Initial instruction has to be followed up with tough simulation, actual communicating, and brutal critique.

As a commander, I went through this sort of training as well as tough prep sessions before press conferences, congressional testimony, and the like. My own public affairs staff, or higher headquarters staff, put me through the ringer, shooting tough questions, trying to confuse or fluster me, and giving hard feedback on my responses and reactions. Not pleasant, but extremely valuable.

NEGOTIATING, MEDIATING, AND FACILITATING

The eight peace mediation efforts I've engaged in—among them the Israeli-Palestinian conflict and long-festering conflicts in Africa and Asia—have taught me the value of expertise in mediating. The ability to arbitrate and negotiate sensitive and adversarial issues is essential to every leader in every field at every level. Conflicts of all kinds have to be resolved. Business deals have to be closed. Contracts have to be negotiated.

In my peace mediation efforts, I learned negotiation, mediation, and facilitation skills firsthand, working closely with expert diplomats, leaders of nongovernmental organizations, and academics. At conferences and retreats with renowned mediators, I have been awed by the depth and complexity of their expertise. All these experts and professionals—both in the field and at conferences—have mastered the art of negotiation to a level I had never imagined.

They know how to keep negotiations focused and on track. They can relate and connect to the parties in order to build the trust and confidence necessary to reach agreement. They understand how to construct innovative structures and components to meet specific needs or bridge gaps. For example, during one mediation effort I was involved in, they created a team of "wise men"—men and women of high stature who could oversee the process and stand above the negotiation but could be called on by either side to move the process forward.

SURPRISINGLY, NEGOTIATING SKILLS have only recently been offered in degree programs at universities. We need many more such programs. Serious conflicts are never going away; resolving them is never easy; and even after their resolution, unhealed wounds may fester for months or years.

Resolving the racial conflict in South Africa, for example, required establishing a delicate environment for reconciliation. Tensions still remain, yet enlightened actions by the nation's leaders have contained what could have been a highly explosive atmosphere and have generated hope for future progress and racial peace.

More attention to an atmosphere of reconciliation early on might have prevented much of the sectarian strife that developed in Iraq.

Leaders who must guide their enterprises through mergers or major downsizing or tough labor versus management disputes must also be able to establish an environment of reconciliation. Constructing and implementing a reconciliation program requires skill in all forms of negotiating and mediating. These skills are another component of the emerging communications requirements for leaders in today's challenging world.

STRATEGIC COMMUNICATIONS

Every organization must develop and then continually question and refine its strategy—its understanding of its purpose, direction, and vision.

An integral part of strategic development is a communications plan to clearly convey both the message of the enterprise's vision, purpose, and direction and its desired image and identity.

Organizations now have expert communications staffs to develop and implement these plans. They build relationships and networks with the media, customers, and all other stakeholders to ensure that all understand the enterprise, what it is doing, and where it is heading.

The last administration established a team in the State Department for strategic communication and promoting a positive image of the United States in a world that was growing ever more unfriendly. The administration was looking for new ways to convey our message.

This effort met with mixed results, despite its well-intended attempts to reach out to other societies where friction points with the United States existed.

IN A GLOBALIZED WORLD, cross-cultural communications are difficult, and competing messages vie for attention. The demand for effective communications and communicators has never been greater. Communicating well is a core leadership competency.

TWELVE

DECISION

Decision making is the soul of leadership. Good leaders know how to make decisions. Good leaders make tough decisions. Good leaders make good decisions.

How do successful leaders make decisions? What goes into making sound decisions? What are the different ways to make decisions? How do decision-making processes work? A lot of observation, thought, and study have gone into answering these questions.

Studies of decision making point out three effective decision-making processes: analytical, recognitional, and intuitive.

Analytical decision making involves careful and detailed examination of all pertinent data relating to the decision. The data is collected, studied, integrated, and evaluated in a way that brings about the most informed decision.

In fields of endeavor with regularly repeating situations and conditions, standardized analytic processes have been developed. In the military we have developed an elaborate analytic planning process for making operational decisions. Our catalogue of the kinds of data and information required for processing and integrating the decision process is based on the study of military history and military experience over—literally—thousands of years.

Recognitional decision making bases decisions on rapid identification of patterns or trends. We make recognitional decisions every day without thinking about it—in driving, for instance. No two driving situations are the same, yet over time and with experience, we internalize sets of patterns that resemble most situations we will encounter: the weather, the layout of the cars, traffic conditions, rates of speed, lights. We process all this data very rapidly and recognize the emerging patterns—when to stop, when to turn, when to slow down, when to speed up, when to stay away from some guy. This is classic recognitional decision making. We see patterns and trends and immediately register decisions and actions. The ability only comes from a great deal of experience.

Modern approaches to decision making work to develop pattern analysis skills in leaders. In today's fast-moving and competitive world, these skills have obvious advantages in speed of decision making and focus on collecting and processing the most relevant data and information. Leaders with recognitional skills know how to glean from experience the core elements needed to make sound judgments. For these reasons, and because recognitional skills can be learned, recognitional decision making has become the mainstay of leader development programs in fields where there is no time for detailed and exhaustive analysis.

Most of us recognize some form of *intuitive decision making*— usually seen as coming out of an instinctive, seat-of-the-pants feeling: "My gut tells me to go this way and not that." Some leaders have an uncanny ability to take a quick read or to sense some intangible element not evident to others that gives them a clear insight to the right call.

Like millions of others, in January 2009 I watched the "Miracle on the Hudson" unfold on TV—the remarkable feats of pilot Chesley "Sully" Sullenberger as he safely landed his stricken airliner in the icy Hudson River and rapidly oversaw the evacuation of all on board. His superb aviation skills saved the entire crew and passengers of U.S. Airways flight 1549. As I watched him describe these events to Katie Couric on *60 Minutes* in February, I couldn't help but think that this man had to be the supreme intuitive decision maker. In three and a half minutes, with no time for analyses or review of options, he intuitively processed forty plus years of experience and study of his profession and calmly made a series of perfect decisions. . . . Any less than perfect decisions would have likely led to the deaths of some or all on board.

How did he arrive at those perfect decisions? What processes passed through his brain? He probably couldn't tell us. But the processes come dramatically alive in the cockpit audio tapes of the three and a half minutes before the river landing. We can hear his cool, steady voice work through the systematic consideration and elimination of options to return to LaGuardia or to try to reach Teterboro, New Jersey (the two nearest airports), while assessing the condition of his engines (both of them were dead), glide time and space, and the best place in the water to set the plane down.

Few of us can become decision makers at the Sully Sullenberger level, but his story clearly demonstrates how analyzed experience, developed skills, and a decisive mind combine to produce a hero in action.

Some people have good intuition. Other people think they do but don't. What's the difference? Can people be trained to become good intuitive decision makers? I'm not sure. But I lean toward doubt.

New leaders in any field are first taught to be analytical decision makers. As they progress and gain experience, they can be trained to become effective recognitional decision makers. A few truly exceptional leaders evolve into superb intuitive decision makers.

Take, for example, quarterbacks in professional football.

The rookie, learning quarterback goes through an analytical process. With clipboard in hand, he plots plays, he listens on headphones to the play selection, he monitors coaches' discussions on the sidelines. He constantly collects data and learns how to process it.

The starting quarterback has gone through that process and often has years of game experiences. He reads patterns in the opposition defenses and sees vulnerabilities, he quickly processes the plays called to him through his helmet receiver, and he makes on-the-field judgments when to call an audible (that is, change the play when he spots an opportunity). He has arrived as a recognitional decision maker.

The Hall of Fame quarterback is the consummate intuitive decision maker. He has the seemingly magical sixth sense that sees opportunities or problems no one else can. He can glance at a single defensive player and understand the defensive scheme he faces.

Good coaches and training programs have developed hundreds of excellent starting quarterbacks, but I don't think training or programs can produce Hall of Famers. You can't mass-produce the level of talent of Johnny Unitas, Dan Marino, or Joe Montana.

That's why I doubt that exceptional intuition can be developed. An element of natural ability is probably necessary in the mix.

GOOD DECISIONS

I have participated in a number of studies and exercises designed to understand how effective leaders make decisions, and I have worked with leader development programs designed to teach decision making. Good decisions can come from any of the three decision-making processes. In my view, good decisions depend less on the process used than on actually understanding the processes and the core elements that go into making good decisions.

Even though that last statement is true as far as it goes, decision makers who quickly analyze data, process it into useful information, and then weave that into a synthesized basis for action succeed today far more often than the slow, the methodical, and the careful. Old systems of staffing and processing information based on careful deliberation and reducing risk may produce more thorough analyses, but fast-hitting events make the results irrelevant. That doesn't mean you shouldn't use as much time for thorough analysis as you have available, but that kind of time is rare.

IF DECISION MAKING IS THE soul of leadership, the soul of decision making is the ability to define the problem.

Overwhelming deluges of data pour in on decision makers, forcing them to make decisions faster than their adversaries or competitors. Competitors will usually have access to the same levels of information—and often to the same information. Whoever effectively processes it faster and smarter wins.

Take an element like weather. In combat, my weather guy processes loads of climatic factors *(data)* about winds, clouds, humidity, precipitation, and air pressure and turns all this into a forecast *(information)*. He then says to me, "Sir, tomorrow there's going to be heavy rains. Dark skies. Thundershowers all day. Poor visibility. Roads will be flooded." Then we examine the forecast in terms of its advantages or disadvantages for military operations *(knowledge)*. The next day, we had planned a mechanized attack down roads that are likely to be flooded. Our ability to use the roads, our ability to resupply, visibility, and many other factors make that kind of attack extremely difficult. It's going to move too slow.

We look at other options: A night attack using infantry may be a better choice. In bad weather, night attacks are much more difficult for the defenders.

Then we choose an operational scheme that exploits the advantages over the enemy and protects against disadvantages to us *(understanding)*.

I've taken climate data and swiftly moved it to a decision that's the wisest available in the environment we face. The process went from data, to information, to knowledge, to understanding. We broke the situation down into its data elements *(analysis)*, then built them into usable elements *(synthesis)* for a sound decision.

I cringe today when I hear the fashionable term "actionable intelligence." This has come to mean that the information itself must provide the action I should take—the decision is inherent in the information. It is an excuse, a copout. The decision is not dictated by the knowledge of the problem or situation. That is only the first step in understanding and decision making. Converting that into wise action involves much more.

HOW DO TODAY'S SUCCESSFUL leaders analyze and define problems faster than their competitors?

They know how to build a bank of experiences, real or simulated, and then draw on them to rapidly recognize and respond to trends and patterns. Relevant experiences come from endless learning, training, and exercises; from the stories and reports of friends and colleagues; from studying the history of their fields; and of course from getting out there and mixing it up in the real world. Rigorous analysis and critique glean patterns and trends from these elements. Recognitional decision-making skills are the end result. Constant practice makes recognitional skills habitual and instinctive.

Pioneers in the study of decision making, such as the late U.S. Air Force colonel John Boyd, have provided powerful insights into that process.

Boyd drew from his own considerable experience as a fighter pilot to describe the decision-making process as a cycle, which he called the "OODA Loop"—*o*bservation, *o*rientation, *d*ecision, and *a*ction. In a dogfight, the fighter pilot who goes through the cycle faster and with more insight wins. Boyd correctly realized that this is true of virtually all decision-making cycles.

Military leaders have institutionalized Boyd's work in leader training programs and in an operational structure that rapidly turns data into information, information into knowledge, and then knowledge into the understanding that grounds sound decisions. During an air campaign where we are attacking targets over a period of time, each series of attacks—or cycle—is broken down into processing intelligence into potential targets, planning the attacks, conducting the attack, and assessing the results. These cycles of attacks are interlocked, meaning that the results of previous attacks are considered in the next attacks. Do we reattack targets not destroyed? Does an unexpected result from a previous attack create an opportunity to exploit in the next attack? In other words, the cycles are joined into an overall systematic process that, if executed more rapidly than the enemy's process, will unravel the opposition's ability to deal with it.

In business, we go through similar processes. We try to field products faster than our competitors; we try to get the jump on innovative technology; we try to close a deal quicker. Producing quality results at a quicker pace is critical to an effective decision process.

While speed and well-oiled processes are vitally important, the centerpiece to the *quality* of the decision is the "orientation" in Boyd's cycle: the ability to instantly define the problem or issue.

In complex military operations, operational commands have to blend large sets of decisions into coordinated and integrated actions. Those air attacks have to be blended with the maneuver of ground forces, the collection and processing of intelligence, the logistics support necessary to sustain operations, and so on. To accomplish this, military commands establish what is called a "battle rhythm," which enables them to effectively manage and integrate the cycles they pass through and allows commanders to control the tempo of operations. That translates into faster, harder-hitting actions than your opponent's.

Battle rhythm operates very much like the inner workings of a classic watch. When you open the watch, you see interconnected gears of all sizes that have to be perfectly synchronized to produce accurate timekeeping. This synchronization is, of course, mechanical and therefore far less complex than the kind of synchronicity we try to achieve on a battlefield or in business, where the processes are more complex and outcomes are harder to predict. In the world of battle or business, we try to link the processes in ways that create a cooperative rhythm that makes us more effective and efficient than our competition.

When the component parts of our processes are not in sync and our rhythm is off, we get bad decisions.

BAD DECISIONS

Bad decisions can result from:

- poor decision structure
- inadequate or poorly processed data

- bias that blinds or limits decision making
- lack of experience and training to recognize trends or patterns
- ineffective assessments of outcomes, stress, or timing
- falling behind the competition's ability to make sound decisions
- failure to accurately identify the problem
- group decision making, or groupthink.

The compromise and consensus required for group decisions frequently produce weak, watered-down, and less-than-clear-cut decisions.

Responsibility for decisions and accountability has to be clearly fixed on the leader. Leaders should not shirk this responsibility or try to pass off tough calls. This invariably leads to bad results. As Harry Truman famously said, "The buck stops here." This doesn't mean leaders should not seek counsel and input or solicit options from others. Sometimes decisions have to be shaped as ideas are processed and clarity is formed. In the end, however, it's the boss who has to make the call, and he has to feel in his gut that it's right.

Other bad decisions are caused by bad assumptions and failure to see a decision's second- and third-order effects. If assumptions are not challenged and minimized, they can become critical flaws in the process. The depth of the problem and the full effect of decisions, particularly those that deal with complex issues, have to be thoroughly thought out. If you don't do that, you can fix one problem and create five more.

THE TARGET OF THE DECISION

Making fast decisions is not enough. They have to be fast decisions at the right time, and their effects have to be focused on the right place.

Every problem, competitor, or enemy has a center of gravity—core strengths and power relative to us, our goals, and our objectives. We need to discover those opposing centers and affect them in a way that is either advantageous to us or at least mitigates their threat to us. The center, or centers, of gravity we choose to affect have to be vulnerable to what we can bring against them; and our actions have to be decisive in resolving the issue. Destruction of a key enemy force, capture of the capital city, fielding a product more innovative and marketable than the competition's, and patenting a unique technology before anyone else does are actions that can successfully attack a center of gravity. The key sequence we need to follow is: (1) Identify the problem; (2) identify the center of gravity we want to affect; (3) identify and implement the action needed. It's not just speed that's important, but the relevant action taken.

It's also important to remember that bold decisiveness unmoored from experience—blind faith in some innate, uncanny ability to make good decisions—is folly. Worse, it is dangerous. It is the quality of analysis that counts in making decisions, not just the willingness to make them boldly and quickly.

PEOPLE DECISIONS

Successful leaders do their best to base choices about membership in their organizations on objective standards that will predict talent, skills, and potential. Human Resources recruiters wade through resumes searching for the best blend of education, talent, and skills; coaches put athletes through physical drills to determine skill levels; and military recruiters put recruits through exhaustive interviews to determine suitability to service. These are all useful systems that provide generally positive results. Yet, no recruiting system provides anywhere near complete satisfaction. No leader will achieve 100% success in choosing the right people.

People are complex and multifaceted, and come with bewildering arrays of strengths and weaknesses that may not be instantly apparent. Highly intelligent people may have no drive. People of only moderate intelligence may dazzle with charm and charisma. Highly skilled and talented star athletes don't always adapt well to team play. Many who may otherwise do okay in military service don't stand up to the stresses and dangers of combat.

Meanwhile, job seekers have learned to game systems to their advantage. Resumes are cleverly doctored to enhance credentials and cloud faults and failings.

At the start of the 2008 NFL football season, the Dallas Cowboys seemed to be the team to beat. They had acquired a dominating phalanx of superstar players. They were a powerhouse team . . . on paper. There was no questioning the raw talent of cornerback and return specialist "Pacman" Jones, of wide receiver Terrell Owens (T.O.), or of quarterback Tony Romo. Yet every sports fan knows that the team everybody picked to reach the Super Bowl failed to even make the playoffs. Soon after the end of the season, the team owner, Jerry Jones, released Pacman, T.O., and other "superstars" who only a few months earlier had been the team's ticket to a championship.

Why? What went wrong? What prevented these truly superstar athletes from achieving their potential—or their team's potential?

Why are people decisions so hard?

Because personality, motivation, compatibility, commitment, integrity, and other factors transcend measurable talent and skills. It's hard to judge these intangible qualities until events and conditions bring them out.

The New York voters who elected Governor Eliot Spitzer or the Illinois voters who elected Governor Rod Blagojevich were clearly shocked to discover that the shining liberal reformers they thought they were electing turned out to be sleazy and immoral. You'd have thought that the rigorous media scrutiny during the brutal campaign process would have spotlighted these character defects. But that didn't happen.

Though leaders will make mistakes in judging people, these are normally mitigated by the better judgment that comes with experience. A leader learns to detect character-revealing signals and the intangible qualities that tests and interviews fail to spotlight.

Choosing good people is not the only people-related decision leaders face. They must also decide what to do when someone isn't measuring up. Offering help (such as counseling or training) is the easy part. It's much more difficult to decide whether or not an individual is salvageable and how hard it will be to salvage him. Can the organization afford the time and effort it would take to bring him around? How will his peers see the investment? Very tough calls.

REVIEWING DECISIONS

How do we shine a clear light on the real causes that make decisions succeed or fail? In the military, we have come up with effective techniques and procedures: no-fault examinations of what really happened, which the Army calls after action reviews (AARs). AAR techniques are no less effective in every other area of human endeavor.

The military has always looked at actions—whether in battle or in training—for lessons learned. Where the stakes are so high, you want to know why things go wrong. But as time passed, the lessons-learned exercise had more often than not become a routine rehashing of events. That changed in the early 1980s, when the Army's Battle Command Training Program (BCTP) took the process to a very much deeper level. (The other services followed suit. The Marine Corps' Marine Air Ground Staff Planning Program, for example, launched a similar effort.)

The programs involve a close, thoughtful, deep, detailed, introspective, extremely rigorous, and *no-fault* analysis of what happened and why it happened during field or computer-simulated exercises. But more than that, they turn a bright spotlight on the leaders and their actions, functions, and decisions. No one from the top down is spared . . . and the examinations can be very tough, the scrutiny can be withering. Yet the aim is not to assign blame or to embarrass any leader. The aim is simply to lay out clearly and analyze exactly what happened—right and wrong—and why.

You look first at the events—all the facts and all the elements—until you reach agreement on what actually happened. Then you closely examine the processes and decisions, and make an assessment of what went right and what went wrong and what caused both. To help you, subject matter experts monitor and critique the rights and wrongs. When anyone points out a mistake or a hole in your decisions, you're allowed to respond, but in a constructive, not whiny, way. You don't make excuses. At the end, you draw lessons.

There's no score assigned. No one gets a grade, passing or failing. No one gets blamed. When I first sat through one of these sessions at Fort Bragg, North Carolina, I watched an Army corps commander, a three-star general, go through a tough recap and critique before all the subordinate leaders of his command, followed by an open and honest self-critique of his own actions. It was clear to me that this process had greatly increased his subordinates' respect for him, and that his unit was made better by it. Ego was out. Learning was in!

An honest and open AAR process can't affix blame. When you affix blame, people will either go into denial and refuse responsibility, or else they'll cover up and won't be open about what happened.

When feedback is given to individuals, there has to be an understanding that it will not become a basis for evaluating performance. That kind of feedback is now a big element in our military culture. In such an environment, you're allowed to fail. You're allowed to make mistakes. In fact, if it looks like you're not making mistakes, not failing in any way, we begin to suspect that you're not really stretching and pushing the edge; or else we're not getting accurate reporting. We expect you to fail at times during training. Failure has to be part of the learning process.

This principle applies to the entire organization. The process should be designed to stress both the organization and its leadership.

When I was a young officer, I used to run tactical tests for infantry companies in our division. These were designed to give company commanders—young captains—an opportunity to test their units, measure their tactical status, experiment with new ideas and methods, and train and develop their leadership. On occasion battalion commanders, observing their companies, would come to me and ask, "How did that captain do? How did he compare with the other captains in the battalion?"

And I would reply, "Sir, I would never answer that. My job is to provide to each captain an evaluation of the performance of his unit and its leaders."

The purpose of the exercise was to discover a company's strengths and weaknesses and then to give the captain an assessment of what he'd done in an open and trusting manner. I couldn't make comparisons or pass on judgments to his seniors. Doing that would defeat the purpose of the training. It would become an evaluation of individuals rather than a means of assessing unit readiness.

We had set up a training environment where we wanted our officers and units to be able to fail, experiment, make mistakes, and be open about what went wrong. We were looking at leadership processes and functions in order to make the organization better. Events were different from company to company. Conditions were different. On what basis could we compare and evaluate performance, even if we wanted to?

In every field, we need to separate programs designed to develop leaders from programs to evaluate them.

Many businesses run so-called leader development programs stacked with exercises and events that are great for improving leadership ability but become tools for evaluation. As a result, they stifle learning. An individual will never approach a learning event the way he approaches an evaluation event. He will approach a learning event with openness, trust, and honesty. He will look carefully at the areas he needs to improve. He will try risky approaches, and he'll be willing to push his limits to the edge of failure and beyond. He will be honest about his shortcomings and open to ways to improve. This won't happen in an evaluation setting. You can't mix the two.

Of course, you can always set up separate exercises, one for training, the other for evaluation. If you clearly understand which is which, there's no problem. "This is going to be an evaluation. You're going to get a grade on it. This is for score, guys." But that's a very different process from training, education, and evolutions that lead to understanding of your actions.

More and more business organizations are basing leader development training on simulated problem-solving experiences followed by constructive feedback. At off-site locations, leaders are given challenging exercises in team building or simulated crises to resolve and then discuss. The organization's problem-solving processes and skills are inevitably greatly improved.

RISK

When I was commander of CENTCOM, from time to time a military strike or operation was contemplated. Before an operational decision was made, I would normally brief the president and the secretary of defense—the civilian leaders who had to make these critical decisions. I was always required by the chairman of the Joint Chiefs of Staff, General Hugh Shelton, to present a risk assessment at these briefings. He put great emphasis on that. He wanted to make sure that our civilian leaders had a full understanding of the complexity and risk of their decisions.

The most difficult decisions all carry forms of risk. Those that carry the highest risk are obviously going to be tough. But if you can define the risk, you have a leg up toward handling it. You will face other tough decisions where the risk is confused or undefinable, so you can't be sure how to deal with them. Sometimes your choices are all high risk and have equally distasteful consequences. You're damned if you do; you're damned if you don't; it's not clear. You can see the advantages and the disadvantages, the dangers and the rewards. But you have no way to discern where the weight of advantages and disadvantages, risks and rewards, falls.

What is risk? How do we measure it?

In the military, decisions with the greatest risk traditionally threaten the survival of your force and/or the accomplishment of the mission. There are ways to categorize and measure risk. What is at risk if I do this? Or that? What is the level of risk? If I fail, what are the consequences? Is the failure catastrophic? What's the level of damage that could come as a result?

Let's say I've been ordered to attack a hill. I know that I need a three-to-one ratio to attack that hill successfully. But I don't have the forces and I can't wait for reinforcements, and the hill is critical terrain that needs to be occupied. So I'm going to ask some unit to make the attack one on one. A tremendous risk. I have to weigh the risk to the unit against the need for that hill.

In business, the military, government, or any field of endeavor, you should have very detailed ways to define risk. It's an essential element of defining the problem.

High-risk decisions in business are not very different from high-risk decisions in the military (although they rarely involve loss of life or destruction of property). Those with the greatest risk threaten the survival of the enterprise.

In business, we're taking a risk every time our company acquires another company and every time we divest some branch of our company; every time we produce a new product; every time we open a new factory, plant, or branch; and every time we enter a new market.

We decide to make a major investment—say, to build that new plant. Our analysis tells us that the new investment will improve our business, but we can't be completely sure.

If the investment turns out to be a loser, what then? Does it risk all our earnings? Could it destroy the business? Could it set us back five years? Could a failure mean that our stock price falls below the level where analysts have faith in the company, and that makes our stock tank?

Sometimes we don't risk enough. In the publishing business, the books booksellers buy are returnable for full credit. That is, the booksellers can send them back to the publishers with no loss to themselves. This is generally a good thing, since publishers want as many books on booksellers' shelves as possible and are generally able to take larger hits than booksellers. But publishers also have good reasons to limit returns (as the books that go back to publishers are called). The more control publishers have over returns, the more they limit them, the more they profit . . . generally.

But there can also be too few returns. That is, publishers will limit distribution so much there aren't enough copies of a book out there on the shelves. Buyers don't see it and can't buy it. The publisher has limited returns, but sells fewer copies of the book than he might have done.

The military tries to limit fighter pilot accidents—for very good reasons! But flying fighter aircraft is an inherently dangerous business, and to be the best in combat, you have to take risks in training. You want zero accidents, of course. But if you get too close to zero, you have to ask yourself if you're training hard enough, pushing the envelope out far enough. A balance has to be struck between acceptable risk and the requirements for critical mission success.

OVER THE YEARS, I've been asked by the U.S. Institute of Peace and other organizations involved in international peace negotiations to join their teams in difficult, high-risk mediation efforts.

In 2002, I joined the Centre for Humanitarian Dialogue in Geneva as part of their team engaged in tough negotiations between the Indonesian government and the Free Aceh Movement, which was seeking independence in the oil-rich province of Aceh on the western tip of Sumatra. When I got on the scene, I quickly became sensitive to the high level of risk each side felt.

For many years, Aceh had fought for independence. But there was simply no way the Indonesian government was going to grant it. Indonesia is a patched-together nation of thousands of islands, many with distinct histories. If one leaves, how many other patches will follow? The nation had recently been through the separation of East Timor and its tragic aftereffects.

I watched the Free Aceh delegates agonize over their choices. Could they accept less than full independence? Even if they could achieve their objectives through some autonomy arrangement, what about the years of sacrifices for independence made by the fighters?

WHEN COLIN POWELL WAS secretary of state, I was asked to help mediate a workable agreement between the Israelis and the Palestinians. In those days, Ariel Sharon was the Israeli prime minister, and the Palestinians were headed by Yasser Arafat. It was fascinating to observe and participate in the interaction between these two strong, difficult, and very different leaders.

The issues were labyrinthine. Many were technical and procedural, and far from easy. And many came out of the core of each side's being and their primal understandings of who they are—issues like national, ethnic, and religious birthright.

Though this seemed deeply out of character for an old, set-in-his-ways warrior like Ariel Sharon, the Israeli prime minister was willing to take risks; he was going through an epiphany. He saw a chance to climb to the top of the mountain. But the political pressures on him were enormous. All the time we were negotiating, Hamas was sending over suicide bombers who were killing innocent Israelis. Every time that happened, Sharon's ability to stay with the process died a little. I watched him go through seven attacks. One time in his office, he took me to a window. "Look out there," he told me. "They march the funeral right beneath my window. They want to make sure I see it. They want me to feel the pressure."

Eventually Sharon could not risk any more, and he broke off the negotiations. Later he took the tough step of removing Israeli settlements from Gaza, a bold move for a man long known as the father of the settlements.

Arafat was not as willing as Sharon to take risks. During one of my conversations with him, he observed what had happened to others who'd taken great risks for peace. Anwar Sadat and Yitzhak Rabin were assassinated. Ehud Barak was politically crushed.

"I'm not going to do that," he told me. "You're not going to walk behind my funeral. . . . I'm still the only undefeated Arab general."

This was his real message to me: Even though he understood that Israelis and Palestinians would in time make compromises and accommodations, he wasn't going to be the Palestinian leader who made them. Those who came after him could do that. He intended to go out of this world with his reputation as uncompromising rebel, leader, and freedom fighter intact. Others could make the compromises, but he couldn't go there.

Nor did he trust that follow-on promises would be kept. If he took the initial risks and made the initial compromises on the Roadmap to Peace (as the United States named the process), what guarantees did he have that the other side would take later, more difficult risks and more difficult compromises?

I'VE BEEN ENGAGED IN numerous situations like these. I've been involved with world leaders deciding on war or peace, testing nuclear weapons, compromising for peace, and engaging in dialogue with old enemies. During these sessions, I could read on every leader's face the churning, internal debate as he weighed risk: personal risk, security risk, risk to national pride, risk to future generations, risk to past sacrifices, and many other kinds of risk.

Leaders are chosen to make those calls; and in the end, they don't get much help in making them. It is truly lonely at the top.

THIRTEEN

CRISIS

Ships hit icebergs. Star quarterbacks break legs. Drought comes; farms fail. New technologies emerge; old industries face collapse. Thousands of homeowners default on mortgages; credit dries up; investments dry up; once-healthy enterprises now face a bleak future.

Crises hit—unexpected events that seriously damage the functions or operations of an organization or a community, or threaten its very existence. You can depend on it. In the military, we constantly talk about the "fog and friction" of war—the unpredictable elements that can make the best plans irrelevant or turn certain victory into potential defeat. Stuff happens.

Change, like crisis, is inevitable. If you lead any organization for any amount of time, you will have to lead it through change. "Change or die" has to be the motto of organizations faced with the stiff global competition and complex environment of today's world. To adapt to an increasingly complicated and changing environment, organizations have to grow, expand, alter, streamline, merge, or divest. The impact of change can be as difficult to manage as the impact of a crisis.

Nothing tests the true character of a leader like leading through crisis and change.

CRISIS

Every organization—whether religious, military, business, nonprofit, or government—will inevitably face a crisis that will test its capacity to steer a safe course through stormy times. Human nature, the nature of the enterprise, the environment, culture, politics, bad luck, or any number of other causes will generate crisis.

Humankind has a wealth of experience facing, surviving, and overcoming—or failing to overcome—crises. Mountains of books, documents, and reports record these experiences; yet organizations and leaders still fall into the traps and mistakes that were made last year . . . or a hundred, a thousand, or ten thousand years ago.

Consultants who specialize in crisis management advice and training do not want for business. In the past, they may have been called in after a crisis has hit, but now savvy organizations bring them in to coach leaders through potential crises before they hit.

We all remember leaders who successfully navigated through times of crisis. Mayor Giuliani in New York on 9/11. National Guard general Russel Honoré and Coast Guard admiral Thad Allen in New Orleans after Hurricane Katrina. Franklin Roosevelt and Winston Churchill in times of depression and war. We also remember those who failed: "Brownie, you're doin' a heck of a job." History clearly shows that the crisis event can make or break the man or the woman.

CRISES DON'T ACCOMMODATE our desires and plans. That's part of what makes them crises. Nor do they come at us politely. They don't give breaks. We think one is hitting us, we think we can handle it; and then we get hit by a swarm.

When the Obama administration assumed the reins of government in 2009, they walked into a swarm of crises. The economy, energy, healthcare, two wars, strained international relationships, and numerous other problems were awaiting the new president and his team the day he took the oath of office.

Obama's approach to these crises offers a fascinating study in how effective leaders face multiple problems.

In putting together his team, President Obama chose as his model Lincoln's "Team of Rivals." He wanted a team with diverse and competing views to ensure he had a full range of options. He did not want to be limited to a narrow set of groupthink alternatives.

Since he wisely understood he couldn't personally focus on all issues equally, he chose to prioritize the problems. The one he chose as his primary focus was the rapidly crashing economy. Few would argue with that choice. Every American is aware of the president's personal commitment to steer the economy out of crisis. Though some criticize his decisions and programs, and their success or failure remains uncertain, no one questions his focus and personal leadership in facing this crisis. President Obama has clearly been in charge and decisive.

Of course the economy was not the only hot issue he faced. How has he initially managed the others?

Let's look at foreign policy. In this area, the president has chosen to delegate responsibility (though no president can totally ignore foreign policy). It's probably the most striking example of his "Team of Rivals" approach.

Critics claim that "Team of Rivals" is much too nice a term for Obama's foreign policy power hitters. Better, they'll tell you, to call them a "Team of Egos." Vice President Joe Biden, Secretary of State Hillary Clinton, National Security Advisor James L. Jones, and a crew of newly minted and powerful "Special Envoys" with very broad responsibilities are all strong personalities with highly credible foreign policy credentials. Strong, talented people can be difficult to lead and to keep on a common track, but if you can do it, the results can be overwhelmingly positive.

Because no crisis lasts forever, and no president can afford to work only one issue, it will be interesting to see how the president chooses to redirect his leadership focus as the economy begins to recover (assuming that it will do that soon). Inevitably, in my view, he will have to shift toward foreign policy. There's too much confusion in all parts of the world; there are too many failing and unstable states; and there are too many opportunities for crises in countries with whom we have highly charged relationships, countries like Iraq, Pakistan, Afghanistan, or Iran—to name a few. Over the course of his presidency, some political crisis, armed conflict, or vast natural disaster is sure to require his personal leadership.

President Obama's approach to multiple problems is a good one. He made the hard decision about setting priorities. He picked his primary focus of personal effort, and he chose strong teams to address the critically important areas that he himself was unable to personally attend to.

Results will show how successful his approach will turn out to be. Will his economic programs work? Will the strong teams that are not under his direct, personal leadership collide and fission? Time will tell.

Yet we have to give him credit for taking decisive steps to deal with multiple and simultaneous crises.

THE POTENTIAL FOR CRISES is greater today than in the past

Problems such as sexual or financial abuses that once were handled internally are often visible today for all to see. Response time becomes critical as attention, pressure, and focus from the outside come far more quickly than in the past. Whatever the cause, a crisis that could threaten the future of the enterprise may result.

A leader has to accept that the crisis may not be the fault of the leadership or the organization. Acts of God can strike. Bad things do happen to good people, and a leader can't just curse the injustice of what hit him.

A media-generated crisis may not be of your own making; yet, paradoxically, that kind of crisis may prove to be especially difficult to work through. Some hotshot investigative reporter may lump you in with others in your industry who have committed gross abuses; or he may tap into disgruntled employees or customers who may twist the truth . . . or lie. I have witnessed both situations. It's frustrating when you do your best to be open and transparent with media and regulatory representatives, and they turn a deaf ear.

Another crisis generator is the worldwide scope of businesses. Most businesses have global tentacles that create support networks that are difficult to monitor. Distributors and suppliers are everywhere. The complexity of the systems is mind boggling. And with it the potential for crisis.

You're the CEO of a company that produces infant formula and pet food, much of which is made in foreign countries, such as China. Your Chinese suppliers contaminate the formula and the pet food with melamine in order to boost their apparent protein numbers. Children and dogs get sick; some even die. Your company falls in a large, dark hole. It was your label on that product.

Your company manufactures furniture, much of which is fabricated overseas. It turns out that many of the laborers there are children. You were getting quality furniture at a reasonable price. You made the contract. But you had no depth of understanding of the labor conditions. And suddenly you are bitten by it.

Other crises can be ignited by failures in internal leadership, ethical behavior, structural flaws, systems, processes, or external circumstances—from the drying up of markets to wars, natural disasters, and other instabilities.

You produce clothing for kids. You trust your factory managers in Asia to watch over quality. They turn out to be taking bribes and accepting shoddy, flammable materials.

Your corporate headquarters gets wiped out by a hurricane.

You're the CEO of an airline that has three bad crashes over a two-month period.

Still other crises can be ignited by the demand for action following industry-wide scandals. The pressure for Congress to clean up the abuses of Enron, Tyco, and other sleazy companies brought forth the Sarbanes-Oxley Act, which generated seemingly endless regulations and public scrutiny, with resulting greater emphasis on ethical behavior and corporate social responsibility . . . and far larger pressures coming from many sometimes surprising directions. Companies are now much more exposed and vulnerable to ethical crises. It's no longer good enough just to say "I'm great. I'm good. I have clean practices. I have ethical leadership." You now have to watch out far more carefully for stuff-happens situations that can catch you up in nasty traps. It's not your fault, you can't see it coming, but you get burned anyway. You're nailed. Or maybe it *was* your fault. Someone in the organization screwed up.

In the military, we have a new term—"the strategic corporal." Because of the nature of military operations and conflict today, a lot more hangs on the actions and behavior of lower-ranking members of the organization than in the past. Everyone's actions, even at the lowest levels, have strategic implications and impact. They come back to you. And they can hurt you bad. You can do tremendous work in some country at every level: Eight brigades are doing good work in Iraq, interacting with the local tribes and trying to put a positive American face on our occupation, and a handful of rogue reservists inside Abu Ghraib Prison destroy everything that we've worked so hard to accomplish.

In World War II, Dwight Eisenhower, leading the European theater of operations, did not have to think much about a corporal in a division who mistreated prisoners. In the overall scheme of things back then, it wouldn't have gotten serious high-level attention. But today, when some sergeant on a street corner in Baghdad or Kabul has a lapse in judgment or behavior, it's in every living room in America. Every blogger has something to say about it. Every newspaper. Every foreign politician with some gripe against America talks about it on national television. It gets global attention. Even though there may be thousands of other "strategic corporals" doing all the right things and proudly representing their country, it will be the rare exceptions that will get attention. The rare bad always gets more notice than the overwhelming good.

WHEN BAD THINGS HAPPEN, leaders can't simply curse bad luck, injustice, or their own actions; they must act to correct the problem . . . or, failing that, to weather it and recover from it. If leaders have built a strong institution on a credible ethical base and if their subordinates trust their leadership, they will have established the foundation they need for guiding their enterprise successfully through the crisis. But there are no guarantees of success.

POINTS OF VULNERABILITY

The Chinese put another 2 million more cars on their highways, and somebody blows up a pipeline in Nigeria. The price of gas all over the United States goes up two dollars a gallon.

A farmer in Mississippi now has to pay 17% of his income to keep his pickup truck and farm equipment going. A factory worker in Riverside, California, has a big mortgage and a 55-mile commute to work. He faces a choice: Pay the mortgage or pay for gas. Interstate truckers are having a hard time making ends meet.

For these people, the rising cost of gas may be a catastrophe. The cost of gas is for them a point of vulnerability.

In every business, we must watch over these points of vulnerability—critical areas whose failure can hurt us; hinge elements that are necessary to our business. Obvious examples of hinge elements are the cost of fuel and transport or of necessary components of our products.

We certainly cannot predict where, when, and how a crisis might hit, but we may be able to mitigate against its effects. We can certainly take a hard look at the internal and external factors that could make us vulnerable to a potential crisis. If we can't control them, we may at least be able to reduce our vulnerability and measure the risk and exposure they threaten.

GETTING THROUGH IT

What qualities mark leaders who successfully guide their enterprises through crises? I have worked with a number of organizations that struggled through deeply traumatic events. From these experiences, twelve qualities or actions stand out. Leaders who get through the crisis best:

1. Recognize and accept the reality of the situation for what it is. Don't fool yourself about the severity of the situation, and don't try to sugarcoat it to the members of organization or to the outside world. By the same token, don't be a Chicken Little. Is the sky really falling? Make a true and honest appraisal about what you face and what the facts and impacts are.

2. Let it all come out; don't be in denial. Bad news doesn't get any better with age. The faster, more honest you get the true story out, the better chance you have of dispelling rumors and creating a positive initial impression with your honesty and transparency.

3. Move quickly and decisively. Your people are traumatized, worried, confused, embarrassed, and emotionally drained. The outside world, including your stakeholders, is barking at your heels. What they all want to see is leadership, someone in charge.

4. Be sympathetic with subordinates and their plight but do not commiserate with them. It's too easy for everyone to start feeling sorry for themselves and to give in to their darkest fears. Feel for what they're going through, but convince them to believe that they control their own fate and have to confront and deal with the problem as a team.

5. See the situation as a challenge, and look for opportunities that might derive from it. Promise yourself and your team that you can come out of this a better organization. Promise the stakeholders that you can learn from the crisis and gain from the experience.

6. Emphasize the value of mentoring and counseling through the crisis. Ensure that all leaders get personally involved in these functions, and get outside help if you and the organization need it.

7. Remain loyal to the institution, and stress that commitment to subordinates. If you've built the morale and teamwork that any good leader should have built, now is the time to tap in to it.

8. In resolving the crisis, do not compromise your standards or ethics. Everything you profess to believe in will be tested, and others will watch to see how strongly you adhere to your code.

9. Perform a deep and broad self-assessment . . . a gut check. This will also provide an opportunity to determine how the crisis is affecting you personally. Don't be reluctant to share your own feelings and get the support you need. You may think you are internalizing all your worries and frustrations, but they may be apparent enough to diminish your leadership.

10. Lead from the front by being visible and in charge. Don't lock yourself away. This is the most important time to be out and about. The captain needs to be on the deck when the battle is being fought.

11. Create as positive an environment as you can. Keep spirits up. Look to ensure that everyone knows they will get through this.

12. Lead through your intellect, not your emotions. Stay even-keeled emotionally and base all your decisions on reason, not feelings. Don't let others lose control or act on their emotions.

On the evening of April 8, 1956, a young drill instructor named Matthew McKeon woke up his platoon of Marine recruits at Parris Island, South Carolina, had them hastily put on their gear, and marched them into the swamps. He led them across a tidal estuary called Ribbon Creek. There was confusion in the darkness of the night, and the crossing turned into chaos. The platoon hit a deep hole no one expected, and six recruits drowned.

Training accidents happen in the military. Though they are rare, the nature of the business is dangerous and risky. Training accidents can be just that, accidents, such as equipment failure or acts of God. Or they can be the result of negligence. They are always thoroughly investigated to ensure problems are corrected and to determine responsibility and accountability. Some also get heavy outside attention, as did the rash of aircraft accidents during testing of the MV–22 Osprey a few years ago.

The Ribbon Creek incident shook the Marine Corps to its bones. It came at a time in the 1950s when military cutbacks were causing every organization and program to come under close scrutiny. The very existence of the Marines was threatened; even President Truman had earlier questioned the need for the Corps.

Fortunately, as often in our Corps' history, Congress continued its unwavering support.

Though the Corps was saved, the incident left deep wounds and drew national media and congressional attention. Articles highly critical of the tough Marine recruit training appeared in *Time* and other publications. Congressional members were all over the commandant of the Marine Corps, General Randolph Pate, to act. He did.

General Pate went immediately to Parris Island and made decisions and took actions, some wise, some not. Before an investigation could garner all the facts, he assumed responsibility for the tragedy and ordered changes in training and complete openness to the media. He expected that these actions would end the crisis. It didn't end. Two camps formed: one staunchly in favor of tough Marine training, the other demanding total reform.

A messy court martial of Staff Sergeant McKeon followed, and the Corps found itself in crisis. Fortunately, the Marine Corps was able to provide the necessary remedial measures that ensured better supervision without reducing the tough training battle-tested veterans believed was required to make Marines.

A book about this incident, *The U.S. Marine Corps in Crisis*, was written by Keith Fleming, a former Marine. It is one of the finest case studies of what can go right and what can go wrong in handling an institutional crisis. It dissected all the personalities, decisions, and events and described classic mistakes and brilliant actions by then little-known leaders whose actions during the crisis propelled them to greater things. I read that book as a mid-grade officer. Its lessons stuck with me.

CHANGE

Crises are not the only generators of chaotic or stressful situations. And they are not the only events that can test the strength of an institution and its leadership. Often severe change is enough to create the same problems. Invariably, change will follow a crisis and compound its impact.

Few people like change, especially older members of an organization. We are by nature creatures of habit. We like stability and predictability. Yet today some organizations accept change, live comfortably with it, or even thrive on it. These organizations are known for their adaptability, risk taking, and innovation, and will always have a leg up on the cautious and reluctant competition.

Though the leadership qualities required for overcoming the negative effects of change are virtually identical to those required for overcoming the negative effects of crisis, additional qualities or actions specifically apply to leaders overseeing an organization going through significant change. The leader should:

- Clearly drive the change process. The boss has to be personally and visibly in charge. His commitment to the process must be demonstrated by his direct leadership through it.
- Articulate the reasons for change, the process that the organization will go through to achieve the objectives of the change, and the time the process will take. Everyone in the organization needs to hear from the leader the why and how.
- Ensure the whole organization is committed, engaged, and onboard with the change. He must be clear about what is changing and what is not. He can allow dissenters to express their views, but, in the end, he must demand cooperation and full participation. He must not tolerate obstructionists.
- Try to create enthusiasm for the change. He should emphasize the benefits and need, and be optimistic about the future. He should manage perceptions regarding the changes, and quickly dispel rumors and negativity.
- Create special teams to oversee significant change processes. He should use the team(s) to quickly identify obstacles and conflicts resulting from change and deal with them. He must also make sure the changes are properly implemented and institutionalized.

The most significant change I have experienced was the development of the all-volunteer military after the Vietnam War. The war was unpopular, the strategy to fight it didn't match the heroic and skilled operational and tactical ability on the ground, and World War II–style conventional forces were attempting to adapt to fighting an insurgency—a difficult change made far more difficult by the social upheaval at home caused by race, drug, and counterculture issues. The conventional, draft military was severely stretched to maintain its primary mission as a bulwark against a potential Soviet threat in Europe while fighting the growing war in Asia. The quality of the military was diminished by programs like Project One Hundred Thousand, which required the military to take on 100,000 recruits from the lowest mental category and, often, with many social, and even criminal, problems. The military soon mirrored the social problems back home.

At the end of the war, the military had survived through the sheer raw leadership of many leaders who courageously took on the societal problems that had infected the troops and maintained military standards and skills, even as they fought the war. They led through the crisis. Though many could not handle the change, the few who could stayed on to restructure our military.

The vision of the new military they proposed was astonishing in its depth and scope: We were looking at an all-volunteer force; we would accept only high school graduates or higher; there would be zero tolerance for drugs; education and development programs would make all ranks far more professional; we would demand a more sophisticated approach to operational skills and become more oriented toward high-technology capabilities; and we would become a much more diverse and integrated organization. America's ethnic and racial makeup would be reflected throughout the ranks.

It was a tremendous risk. Many thought it couldn't be done: "You can't recruit the numbers required." "You can't afford the force." "You can never get the popular support for it."

But visionary leaders from all the services committed to it. And those of us who came into the military before and during Vietnam not only witnessed the changes, we lived them and quickly came to appreciate and admire the leaders who stayed the course and created the magnificent military we have today.

WHAT DOES IT TAKE?

Leaders who get us through severe crisis and change have several traits in common.

They are, first and foremost, exceptionally competent. They know their business. They cannot just be cheerleaders. They have to possess the true skills to make the right choices. They have also gained the respect and stature that instills trust and confidence among those they are leading through a trying period. Doubts are overcome by the belief that the leaders will succeed. And, finally, they share and understand the burden. They care about the effects of the crisis on their people, but they don't accept excuses. They lead when true leadership is most needed.

FOURTEEN

VISION

Leaders lead people and organizations toward some goal. Sounds obvious, right? Try asking leaders you know what that goal is. Very few leaders today have a clear vision and a strategic design for achieving it. Very few leaders, in other words, are strategic thinkers.

Strategic thinking and planning have become a lost art. Yet the art is increasingly important. It's harder than ever to succeed without it.

During his 1988 campaign for president, someone urged George H. W. Bush to pay more attention to longer-term objectives and to setting forth inspiring national goals. "Oh, the vision thing," Bush responded dismissively ... as though such things are airy window dressing and don't really matter. Bush was a pragmatic, low-key man, intelligent and competent. But he didn't get "the vision thing." When he was elected president, the Cold War was ending and the strange, much-less-ordered new world we live in today was beginning to evolve. The nation and the world were hungry for vision. Bush lost the 1992 election to Bill Clinton in part because of his failure to articulate and implement a national vision for this new world.

But Bush isn't the only national leader who has failed to articulate a vision. You have to go back to the 1940s and the great strategic giants, George Marshall and George Kennan to find creators of a real and viable national vision and strategic design. Marshall and Kennan understood the challenging world environment our nation then faced—the emerging Cold War; they foresaw its later developments; and they brilliantly articulated and launched the plans and programs needed to meet the challenges.

But we launched into the confused post–Cold War era as a short-attention-span society with a shallow focus on the here and now. Our leaders lacked the ability or will to think through the new challenges we faced and develop the strategic course we needed to take. This has cost us. We can see the disastrous results in our foreign policy, in our handling of conflicts and natural disasters, in the managing of our economy and businesses, and in just about every other way we go about leading our society into the future.

There is a desperate need to face the future and learn, or relearn, how to think and plan strategically.

Where are the Marshalls?

Why don't we make them anymore?

Not long ago, we witnessed the CEOs of the three major American automobile companies come hat in hand before the U.S. Congress to beg for a bailout. This industry has been a poster child for lack of vision, failure to develop a credible strategic design, and inability to understand its environment. One or two or maybe all three of these long-standing, seemingly permanent fixtures in our economy may fail. During 2008, airlines failed . . . or else merged in desperation. Banks were sick or dying. Once-solid companies in other industries were teetering over open graves.

One or two rare companies in these sick industries will succeed. Why? Because they are led by people who use a different approach to doing business and reach more credible visions through well-thought-out planning and direction, and by sensing opportunities and challenges. They are the rare Marshalls we are desperately seeking.

When I joined the Marine Corps, I was taught how to command relatively small units. I learned how to get squads and platoons to accomplish their assigned missions. I was taught tactics. Tactics deal with the short term, the here and now. You attack a hill, you defend a piece of terrain, or you conduct a patrol. I knew all these tactical actions were part of a larger scheme, and I knew that above the tactical level was the operational level and above that the strategic level. From my perspective at the bottom looking up, I imagined that I might be required to master the other two levels if I someday moved up the ladder of increasing command responsibility; but I never imagined that operations and strategy were so significantly different from tactics. As my young mind saw it then, operations and strategy were just larger-scale ways of getting things done. I thought, in other words, that the operational level was just tactics on steroids, and strategy was just operations on steroids.

As I grew into higher command, I learned otherwise.

My first experience commanding at the operational level (preceded by serious education in the operational art) made me realize it was a wholly new and different realm from tactics. I was conducting business over a far greater expanse in time and space, and I was orchestrating and integrating many more military capabilities—such as aviation, logistics, civil affairs, and psychological operations—than I had been used to dealing with. Unlike the relatively sequential way tactical actions were done, many sets of complex actions needed to be done simultaneously. I was putting together complicated tactical events in time and space in order to accomplish a higher set of objectives, and I was shaping future operations while conducting current ones. Planning for and conducting operations during conflict means stringing together a series of battles (tactical events) into a campaign (operational event).

Graduation to the strategic level involved mastery of even more complex skills. The integration required at this level means blending together military and nonmilitary capabilities. All the elements of national power—diplomatic, economic, military, informational, and cultural—must be brought together in a coherent manner to achieve broad, long-range objectives. This requires a very long-term time horizon. It means stringing together campaigns to win wars. It means setting in play the means to establish long-term security relationships through international engagement and partnership building.

The U.S. military system of education and planning, which has functioned at the tactical, operational, and strategic levels for many decades, emerged most notably during and after World War II, when we truly stepped onto the world stage as a superpower.

The other agencies of government don't operate that way. Our partner agencies responsible for nonmilitary functions have either lost the ability to think and act strategically or else they have failed to evolve as the world became more interconnected. This is no less true of most of the private sector.

That's why the military finds itself involved to such a surprising extent in the planning and execution of nonmilitary operations in Iraq and elsewhere.

Most of our government operates on a transactional basis, from day to day. But not only our government; most businesses and most governments in the world operate on a transactional basis. We tend to go from event to event, from transaction to transaction (pure tactics), without clear direction or purpose. This has gotten our society in deep trouble.

And it has not gone unnoticed. People are hungry for vision.

They are looking for a renaissance in strategic thinking . . . expressed in the trendy branding of just about everything as "strategic." We talk about strategic thinking, strategic communications, strategic character, strategic culture, strategic vision, strategic art, strategic leadership, and so on. Though much of this talk is confused and disjointed, it signals a recognition of the need for leading strategically.

What does that mean?

STRATEGIC THINKING

If I were to advise a young aspiring leader about making himself more effective and attractive to his bosses, I would recommend demonstrating his ability to think and analyze over a very wide range. He should be able to clearly describe his environment, to see and articulate future positions for his enterprise in that environment, and to set a course for his enterprise to achieve success. In other words, he should demonstrate that he is a strategic thinker.

Strategic thinkers—whatever their field—grasp what's going on around them in deeper and wider ways than others in their field. They see the complexity and totality of their world more fully than their colleagues or competitors. They get the big picture. They even seem to see into the future—not because they're clairvoyant, but because they have a future orientation. They recognize the opportunities and obstacles that lie ahead, and they know how to effectively and efficiently steer a course through the obstacles and challenges. They have the uncanny ability to drive rather than react to events.

They are members of the rare breed who succeed in fields littered with failing enterprises directed by leaders who repeat the failed processes of long-outdated models.

Congressional committees, an angry public, and an aggressive media, fed up with government officials and overpaid executives who lead failing organizations into catastrophic holes, have begun to fight back. But the officials and executives still seem as oblivious as ever. They have no clue that their failure is based on lack of strategic leadership.

STRATEGIC DESIGN

It's not enough, however, for a true leader to be a strategic thinker. He must also be a strategic *doer*. It's fine to see things in a strategic context, but you also have to tell me what to do about what you see. Consultants can come into an organization and help the leadership think and see strategically, but in the end the leadership must plot the course and sail the ship toward its destination. This process requires planning and design.

I have developed strategic designs for organizations I have led, and I have coached senior leaders through developing a strategic design. It's not easy.

You have to begin with a clear assessment of your operating environment—the world where you do business. You can't take a journey unless you first know where you are starting from and the environment you face during the journey. Believe it or not, many leaders want to launch before they have a clear understanding of the true nature and makeup of their organization, how it fits in its world, and what that world is all about.

Armed with that understanding a leader can then take the next—and most difficult—step of this journey: defining the destination.

VISION

An enterprise's destination, or vision, should be articulated in clear, simple, and credible terms. It is a statement describing the end state a leader envisions after proceeding on the course he and his organization will embark on. It should describe a position the organization will reach in time.

Vision statements can take more than one form. Some may simply describe a percentage of market share to be achieved by some date. Others may describe a set of desired capabilities. Whatever form it takes, the statement has to lead to a strategic plan mapping how to get there. That is, it has to contain real meat. Vague, ambiguous, or airy statements—such as "We will be recognized as an industry leader in five years"—don't get it. Neither does a simple statement of values.

One criticism of national security strategies of past administrations has been that they are nothing more than statements of values and principles. Such statements may be a useful part of a strategic design in that they help identify what you are or aspire to be, but this can't be the total strategy.

Some leaders or consultants get hung up on the length of the vision statement. I don't. As I said, it should be simple. But it doesn't have to start out that way. I'd rather a leader lay out his full thoughts and then work to simplify, condense, and refine them later.

Other leaders, especially those new to the vision-making process, often get sucked into execution of the vision—the how, the ways, and means—before they have actually articulated the vision. They need to be coached into backing off of that and letting the how evolve from the planning that follows.

Thinking through the vision is a tough process. As a leader is forming his vision, he shouldn't be constrained by expectations about the right or wrong way to do it. He should think broadly as he launches into this difficult and critical stage of his strategic design.

STRATEGIC GOALS

After we achieve a strategic vision, we have to determine the practical steps we need to accomplish in order to make the vision a reality. These are our goals.

Let's say our vision statement lays out a percentage of the market we want to achieve over a given period. Those tasked with laying out the goals may come up with this: "Increase the sales staff to reach and service the larger market share." Or: "Add to the product line so as to appeal to a broader market."

Collectively, the goals must add up to the vision. Achieve the goals, and you achieve the vision.

UP TO THIS POINT in our strategic design, we have been working at the strategic level. But just as in the military structure, strategy must drive operations and tactics. The vision and goals give us operational direction, but we can't get there without detailed, nitty-gritty ways and means.

OPERATIONAL OBJECTIVES

Leaders and staff from each part of the organization must now examine what they must do to fulfill their role in making the strategic goals a reality. They set detailed operational objectives at their level that will marry objectives from other parts of the organization. When all these objectives are achieved, the enterprise will achieve its goal and vision.

If we decide to increase our market share by increasing our sales staff, what might that mean practically? Our human resources department may decide we need more sales representatives. That means it will have to increase both the recruiting objective and training. The facilities department may decide to acquire and open new sales offices.

We make the objectives happen through operations and tactics.

Each element of the organization lays out the actions required to gain the objectives. In other words, each objective has an action plan that describes the programs, projects, processes, and steps that will make it happen.

At this point in the strategic planning process, the elements of the organization should be reaching agreement on what is needed to reach the destination the leadership desires. We should now clearly see the company's vision, the goals necessary to get there, and the detailed objectives and action plans from each component of the organization that get us to the goals.

RESOURCE ALLOCATION

There's an old saying in the military attributed to General Omar Bradley: "Amateurs talk tactics; professionals talk logistics." In other words, great ideas are only as good as your ability to achieve them, and your ability to achieve them is dependent on your ability to afford them. When our strategic plan has reached the point where we can see what we need to do to get there, it's time to determine how much it will cost. The cold realities of cost may then cause us to go back and make changes. We may have to adjust our time horizon or lower our expectations. Priorities will, no doubt, have to be set and resources shifted. Decisions about risks of borrowing, restructuring, or streamlining may have to be made so we can actually provide the resources necessary to reach our vision.

So far we have laid out the course. We have a plan. The leadership can clearly see the ends, ways, and means. But the process can't stop here. The design is not complete. We can't throw a plan out to the organization and simply say "Do it."

STRATEGIC STRUCTURE

I have seen organizations painstakingly develop a great plan but fail to provide a structure to oversee the process. Why do we need a structure?

First, we have to be able to look across the whole organization to ensure that every part of it is on track and in sync. We also need to see where problems may be developing in order to address them before parts of the plan lag behind or get out of sequence. Day-to-day operations and decisions have to be weighed against the strategic plan. Are new opportunities popping up? Are challenges or obstacles developing? Is the environment changing? Close monitoring and assessment is critical to staying on course or making decisions to adjust course.

A good strategic plan identifies decision or review points in the course of implementation. Some organizations establish fixed strategic assessment sessions where progress in reaching goals is reported to the leadership in a preset way. Measures of effectiveness or other indicators determine how well the strategic plan is being implemented. Sometimes the goals and objectives are portrayed graphically. For example, a traffic-light model will show green, yellow, or red, depending on how well the plan is working. If the rating is yellow or red, the rationale for the rating is thoroughly briefed to the leadership, and a corrective action plan is presented to them.

These formal processes, together with the depth of attention by leadership, give substance and seriousness to the strategy. The whole organization has to pay attention. Accountability, oversight, and leadership reporting requirements focus and energize the organization.

When I commanded U.S. CENTCOM, a strategic planning element in my staff tracked our progress, but another element also monitored how our day-to-day operations affected our strategy. This check was necessary to make sure our direction remained on course in our highly active, volatile, and crisis-prone environment.

Smaller organizations may need no more than a handful of people to monitor and oversee the strategic design, or even only a single monitor, but it's a rare organization that can sail a coherent and consistent strategic course unguided and unmonitored.

A LOT OF SWEAT goes into strategic planning. Sometimes the effort becomes so consuming that the leadership gets too committed to it and misses changes, opportunities, and challenges.

The process has to remain dynamic.

We must never forget this truth: Leaders can't fall in love with their plan. They must balance creating and achieving the strategic vision and recognizing and dealing with real conditions as they actually emerge.

WHEN GENERAL PETE SCHOOMAKER took over as Chief of Staff of the Army several years ago, he established a course on strategic thinking for his general officers. The course had two points of focus: (1) to enhance his generals' strategic education, and (2) to openly discuss, plan, and assess the United States Army in a strategic context. This last focus provided General Schoomaker with valuable feedback on the strategic direction of his service.

I was privileged to attend and address these warriors on a number of occasions. Their enthusiasm, interest, and insight were truly impressive.

The initial sessions for new generals included discussions of the strategic history of the service, past strategies, strategic thinking, current strategic environment, strategic communications, and strategic character. At later sessions, General Schoomaker's strategic vision was opened for feedback and debate. His successor, General George Casey, has wisely continued this effort.

I came away from the sessions with a real appreciation for all the ways developing strategic leaders can pay off for the organization. We can certainly see its benefits in the performance of these military leaders in today's complex conflicts.

The old saying "If you don't know where you're going, any path will get you there" characterizes many of our institutions and enterprises.

We need leaders more than ever who can think and act strategically. We have to find and develop them better than we have been. Those abilities and skills shouldn't be rare.

MAKING A STRATEGIC PLAN . . .
AND MAKING IT WORK

At DynCorp International, one of my first jobs was to come up with the strategic plan for the company . . . an extremely complex analytical and decision-making process. I had to look at how we were going to grow and enhance the business in the face of very tough and competent competition.

Any leader who aims to develop a strategic plan for his organization will go through a similar process.

As a government services business, DynCorp bids on government contracts, primarily in support of the Departments of State and Defense.

When I started thinking about the plan, I was starting from scratch. I had no previous direct experience in that kind of business. But as I probed deeper, really down into the nitty-gritty analytical work on the company and the market, I began to develop greater understanding . . . and, of course, many very smart and experienced people were helping me. "I don't know a lot about this business," I said to myself. "I don't have a lot of experience. But it strikes me that we have to get right three things—three centers of gravity for our business, three core elements that we must make work well if we are going to make this enterprise successful. Get these three centers of gravity right and our business will improve. First, we have to put a quality proposal on the table when we bid on a contract. Second, we have to define our core competencies, our signature capabilities, and be the best of breed in these key areas necessary for success in this business. Third, we have to put top-quality people out in the field managing. If we put our priorities into these three areas, we will succeed in growing this business."

THE FIRST CENTER OF gravity is quality proposals. There is no barrier to entry in DynCorp's business. A lot of people can enter it. The competition is legion. It's much like the airline industry. If you have the money, and you want to get into it, you can. You just need to hire the right people . . . or hire them away from other successful companies. So we had to make sure that any proposal we presented was first class and prepared by first-class people who knew the process well. When government experts look at proposals (they judge proposals from as many as a dozen companies), they're looking for many facets, skills, innovative approaches, and capabilities, including but not limited to price. According to popular myth, the company that comes in with the lowest bid gets the deal. Not true.

But pricing is obviously important. Experts in our organization would look at the requirements for the work and look at what we had to do to fulfill them—acquire equipment, hire labor, provide a management team. Perhaps we had to transport equipment. Or we had to build a base camp in Afghanistan. Our experts knew how to get these things done; and they knew the prices, the cost of the labor, and where to obtain greater efficiencies. They would come up with our best competitive pricing.

They were extremely important people. If we got the pricing wrong, or if we were trying to do things our competitors could do more efficiently, we were going to lose out. So pricing is a key part of the proposal process.

Also important in building a quality proposal is value: What value do we bring? Can we deliver it? Does our past performance guarantee that? Can we offer innovative methods and approaches that the other bidders can't?

For example, we bid on a security contract in Afghanistan where we offered something unique and proprietary. Our people in Afghanistan would not just be training local police; they would go through a course on cultural sensitivities—understanding their role out there, understanding how their actions could have negative effects, and understanding how to make a positive effect in supporting our government's objectives. We included that in our proposal to demonstrate our understanding that this aspect is key to training success.

Or when we bid on a maintenance contract, we included in our bid an innovative proprietary software program on maintenance management that gave us a competitive edge.

The second center of gravity is knowing and nurturing your own best skill sets—the skills you concentrate on and in which you could be the best of the breed. DynCorp may have been capable of doing, say, twenty things well. I knew we couldn't be better than all of our competitors in all twenty. But because of past performance and the contracts we wanted to win, we could focus our energies on, say, five of the twenty where we could outshine everybody else . . . where we could be the iPod or the iPhone. When we went to make a proposal, these five skills would truly say DynCorp; these were what we're truly known for, the heart of our business. For DynCorp, at the time, the top skill sets included construction management, training of police, drug eradication, fighting wildfires, security, logistics, and air support.

Pick your best. Don't pick too many. Concentrate on them. Get them right.

The third center of gravity is program managers in the field, the guys who run things at the scene. Because DynCorp operated all over the world, the people in charge on the scene could make or break us. Program managers were the most important people in our system of business; they had to be top.

If I looked at our industry's past problems, they were almost always a consequence of the failure of a program manager in the field. Failure had many possible causes—the guy might be incompetent, abrasive, didn't relate well to the customer, didn't adapt to the local culture and mores, or didn't bring the right set of skills . . . or frequently a combination of these.

We created new programs at DynCorp to recruit and train our program managers. We put in a training program where one did not exist before. We beefed up our screening and started screening for things we didn't screen for before. We also sought more customer feedback to ensure our performance in the field met their demands, and we assigned senior regional leaders to oversee our efforts in areas where we had large numbers of contracts and people. This allowed for on-site corporate-level leadership and immediate interaction with the customers on scene.

The three centers of gravity turned out to be the right call.

WE COULDN'T JUST BUILD a plan and stop there. We had to implement the plan—turn it into achievable programs.

For example, because I believe proposals and their preparation are key, we had to establish the right process to develop them, build proposal centers, hire the right consultants, and convince the CEO to put his money into these efforts. We needed to invest in the total process in order to get it right.

And then we had to bring in quality people to fill the key roles: capture manager, proposal manager, the people who ran the proposal centers. And we had to train them. They had to move through the analytical and the recognitional phase; a few of them could make the intuitive phase. We worked all these processes hard. We worked them until we could say, "I've got the 95 score proposal I can put on the table."

We did the same in developing our signature capabilities and the same in recruiting and training the program managers.

THOUGH STRATEGIC THINKING—and strategic doing—have never been easy, in our increasingly turbulent times it's hard to imagine how they could ever have been harder.

The overwhelming strategic reality hanging over most of my life was the Cold War. In those days the consequences of bad choices based on inadequate strategic vision could have been horrendous. Today, when the Cold War is not even a memory for most young people, we face threats not so much to the survival of the planet or of humanity itself, but to our jobs, to our businesses, and even to major industries.

As I write, sober and thoughtful people seem riddled with anxieties about the possibility that the entire global economy might crash. Very unlikely! Yet the course ahead for all of us is stormy and uncertain. The skies above are dark, threatening, and torn by lightning.

How must we plot that course?

We don't need airy dreams masquerading as visions. We need a tough, deep, sharp charting of the way ahead—with the right commitment, resource allocation, and other serious components behind it.

AFTERWORD

People are desperate for leadership they can trust and depend on. They want role models who earn their respect and can get them through tough times.

In this book, I've provided readers with my observations on leadership looking back on almost a half century of experience and looking forward to challenging new times for emerging leaders. I'll sum up with some advice to young men and women seeking to lead.

First, define yourself and your code for living and leading. Never betray your code. Live it, and seek to live a life that matters to you. Think about what you want to leave behind—your legacy. Fight your devils and be true to yourself. Balance your life so that you are a complete, multidimensional person. Challenge yourself to the fullest so you know your full strengths and limitations. Be okay with who you are. Value your word and your words, and never compromise your integrity. Be open to feedback and counsel.

As a leader, be as competent in your field as you can be. Never stop learning. Be smart and decisive, and lead from the front. Use the authority of your position as a last resort. Share your power and trust with those who earn it by inviting them to participate in leading and deciding.

Create a positive environment for your people and care for their welfare. Be a teacher and a mentor. Listen to those you lead, reward them when they perform, relish their diversity, help them when they fail, assist them in their growth and development, and know who they are.

Know what you lead—its every component, part, and function. Provide the vision and direction that makes your organization a success. Create a sense of ownership for all those who are part of the success. Be visible, accountable, and in charge in times of crisis and change for your enterprise. Master time and technology—don't let them drive or control you.

A strange new world has been emerging out there for the last two decades. No one is sure where it is heading. Many fear its challenges, but we need leaders who see its opportunities. Be one of them.

INDEX